The Challenge of the Atlantic

The Challenge
of the
Atlantic

Man's Battle with the World's Toughest Ocean

Dag Pike

Foreword by Richard Branson

Patrick Stephens
Wellingborough, Northamptonshire

British Library Cataloguing in Publication Data

Pike, Dag
The challenge of the Atlantic.
1. Voyages and travels 2. North Atlantic Ocean
I. Title
910'.091631   G540

ISBN 1-85260-002-0

*Patrick Stephens is part of the Thorsons Publishing Group,
Wellingborough, Northamptonshire, England, NN8 2RQ*

Printed in Great Britain by Hazell Watson and Viney, Aylesbury, Buckinghamshire

1 3 5 7 9 10 8 6 4 2

Contents

Acknowledgements

My thanks are due to the following for help, advice and pictures: Alan Brunton-Reed of Thomas Reed Publications Ltd; *Western Morning News*; Frank O. Braynard of American Merchant Marine Museum; Bristol City Archives; New York Public Library; Bristol City Library; Boston Public Library; Liverpool Maritime Museum; The Editor, *Sea Breezes* magazine; US Coast Guard Archives, Washington; Swan Hunter Shipbuilders Ltd; E. H. Cole; Blohm & Voss AG; British Transport Docks Board; Mystic Seaport Museum; Neptune Yachting Magazine, France; Royal Western Yacht Club; Tim Severin; Colin Mudie; Enda O'Coineen; Dr Bob Magoon; Jim Wynne; BMW Marine; Volvo Penta; Richard Branson; Harland & Wolff Ltd; Kate Dinn of Falmouth Art Gallery; Gina Haines, my secretary; *Yachts and Yachting*; Peter Gilson, Royal Cornwall Polytechnic Society.

Foreword

by RICHARD BRANSON

I know from personal experience what the Atlantic can be like. When we made our first attempt on the Atlantic record in 1985 we really thought we had the ocean beaten, until, with only three hours to go, the Atlantic won. *Virgin Atlantic Challenger* became one of the long list of Atlantic casualties.

The next year, we tried again and won and became part of the fascinating history of the Atlantic which Dag Pike has set out so well in this book. The Atlantic is a fantastic challenge ground rivalling Everest as a field of human endeavour, and even with modern technology it is still a tough test of man and machine.

When we completed our successful crossing in *Virgin Atlantic Challenger II,* I threw out a challenge to other teams to attempt to break our record. I am pleased to see that this challenge is being taken up. I am also pleased that Dag Pike has recorded our place in the story and I commend this book to all those with an interest in achievement and history.

Winds, currents and wild seas

The horizon seemed to be playing tricks: it rushed up to meet the mast as the ship rolled over, further and further. The mast seemed intent on matching the line of the horizon and only slowly, ever so slowly, did the roll stop and the ship hang for what seemed an eternity before mast and horizon parted company and started to restore their normal relationship.

It was a heart-stopping, knuckle-whitening moment as the ship fought for survival against the elements intent on its destruction. There was nothing we could do. To fill the ballast tanks would have created a free surface below which would have only made matters worse; perhaps such an act would have been the straw which might have broken the camel's back. Trying to shovel the sea of grain which filled the holds back into its rightful position would have been futile, since the shifting boards erected to keep the grain in place were now lying in a tangled and useless mess.

For 36 hours the ship fought for its life out there on the lonely Atlantic, a battle made the more critical by the fact that her sister ship had capsized and sunk, having lost a similar fight only months before. As a young apprentice, ignorance, perhaps, stopped me from recognizing all the potential consequences of what was happening, or perhaps it was a form of fatalism inherited from generations of seafarers who have taken on the Atlantic and either won or lost at the whim of a capricious mistress.

Gradually the storm eased and the cargo ship *Marjata*, bound from Galveston to Liverpool, lived to fight another day. On one level, she became just another statistic, and a not very important one at that, a vessel whose cargo had shifted in heavy seas, amongst the thousands of ships which have got into difficulties in the North Atlantic. On a personal level the experience of spending 36 hours not knowing whether the next minute would be your last was one which was going to live with me throughout my seafaring days. It taught me respect and humility for the sea and it gave me an understanding of how centuries of seafarers, most of them far less well equipped than we were to cope with the situation, have battled with storms on the Atlantic.

Certainly the experience taught me to regard with due reverence the Western Ocean, a wild stretch of sea which has been both a route for com-

A large French trawler in a North Atlantic storm (Author).

merce and a barrier to trade for several hundred years. Even in modern times the Atlantic still takes its toll: one of the latest mysteries is the loss of the modern container ship *Munchen*, apparently overwhelmed in mid-Atlantic for all her modern equipment. The Atlantic has been, and is still, a challenge to new maritime developments and technology, but above all the ocean is a test of seamanship. It is an ocean which has many changing moods, sometimes calm, but more often rough and occasionally possessed of the most blind and senseless violence. While sailors may call her 'The Pond', with typical understatement, no seaman worth his salt is going to take the Atlantic for granted.

There was a time, so the geologists would have us believe, when the Atlan-

tic wasn't there. Long before history began there was a single large land mass on earth from which the continents as we know them today slowly separated out. This movement continues today at an infinitesimally slow but measurable rate, the chain of volcanic activity running down the centre of the Atlantic being visible evidence of shifts and change in the Earth's crust. Perhaps legends of the lost lands of Atlantis represent dim, distant folk memory of such times but the main visible changes in the Atlantic are not those affecting the land features on the ocean's rim but those arising from the daily, sometimes hourly, change in the sea and the weather which can affect the largest and stoutest of modern ships.

It is the wind which is the main cause of waves at sea and the waves which create most of the problems for shipping, but these elements are just two of the many factors which can make the sur-

Rough seas in the Atlantic from a large freighter (Author).

face of all the oceans such wild and inhospitable places. The North Atlantic, like other seas, is a constantly churning, constantly moving body of water with ocean currents shifting huge volumes of water in three dimensions. Added to this mixture of wind and water are the hazards created by fog and icebergs so it is easy to see why the Atlantic Ocean has established a fearful reputation and why it has been so respected by seamen throughout the ages. The Plimsoll line painted on the hull sides of all cargo ships is an indication of this respect. It appears as a series of horizontal lines which show how deeply the ship can be loaded and was introduced in the 18th century to prevent ships from being overloaded by unscrupulous owners seeking higher profits. A series of lines is necessary to allow for different water densities and different sea conditions with the top line allowing for a deeper draft in less dense

fresh water. Then come load lines for normal summer and winter use, and right at the bottom is a line marked with the letters WNA, standing for Winter North Atlantic. This is the only sea region having its own special load line and is a reflection of the awesome sea conditions which can be found during this season in the North Atlantic. Here the authorities have decreed that extra safety margins are required in order to ensure the safe conduct of shipping.

The Atlantic has earned itself this reputation over the centuries as trade routes have developed across the globe. This ocean has taken a higher toll of shipping than any other and not solely because of the density of shipping crossing the stretch of water between the Old and the New Worlds. Initially the dream of European sailors was just to find what lay on the other side of the great oceanic divide. Then it was the prospect of riches

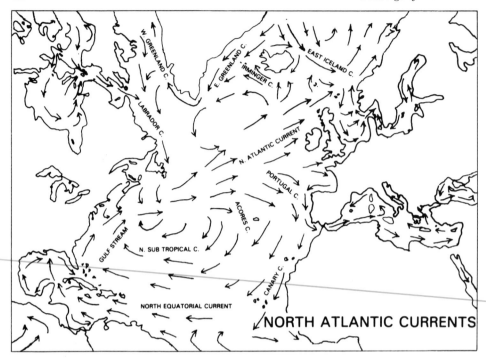

Ocean current circulation in the North Atlantic dictated the routes followed by most sailing ships (Reeds Ocean Navigator).

heating effect of the sun, the air at the Equator would rise as it became heated and this warm upper air would then flow northwards and southwards towards the poles, with colder air from the poles flowing equatorwards to take its place. This north/south air flow is the basic pattern in the Northern Hemisphere but the Coriolis effect caused by the spinning of the earth swings the wind to the right in its southward (equatorward) flow and in fact tends to set up a circular flow of air around the Atlantic.

An area of high pressure (descending air) which builds up around 30°north of the Equator is known as the Horse Latitudes. At latitudes above this area the wind tends to flow to the northeast away from the high pressure, creating the prevailing south-westerly winds which are such a feature of the North Atlantic weather up to about latitude 60° north. Here these south-westerly winds meet up with the north-easterly winds flowing down from the polar regions and it is this meeting of the cold, dry north-easterlies and warm, moist south-westerlies which causes much of the bad weather in the North Atlantic. The meeting line between these two systems is the breeding ground for the depressions which are a constant feature of Atlantic weather and which generate most of the violent winds in the region.

The meeting line between these winds will vary according to the season, moving north in the summer and drifting south in the winter. The drift south in the winter brings the area of violent winds right across the major trade routes and helps to give the North Atlantic the fearsome reputation discussed earlier. The deeper and more violent depressions produce winds which quickly reach gale force or more. Most of the depressions which roll in across the Atlantic are formed over the North American mainland and by the time they reach the ocean, usually around Newfoundland in the summer and further south, perhaps at New York or Cape Hatteras, in the winter, they have developed sufficient intensity to be a hazard to navigation.

In northern areas of the Atlantic then, the general pattern of the weather shows a series of depressions running across from west to east, whilst further south, the Azores high pressure area represents the high pressure of the Horse Latitudes. If the Azores high strengthens, it pushes the depressions further north and this can bring fine weather to most of the maritime routes across the Atlantic. More frequently this high pressure area is beaten south and it is rarely able to fend off for long the assault from the depressions, determined in their eastward path across the North Atlantic.

To the south of the Horse Latitudes, towards the Equator, the wind flow is generally in the opposite direction, sweeping clockwise around the Azores High. This gives us the north-east trades which are the dominant feature of the southern part of the North Atlantic, providing the consistent fresh winds so favoured by sailing ships. Below the Equator, matching these north-easterly

Icing is a hazard in the northern regions (Author).

Above *The Atlantic takes its toll—the wreck of the* Arco Merchant *on the Nantucket Shoals* (US Coast Guard).

Below *The Atlantic at war—battleships fighting the common enemy, rough seas, in World War 2.*

trade winds of the northern hemisphere, are the south-easterly trades which sweep up from south of the Equator on a seasonal basis. In between these two wind systems are the Doldrums, an area of fitful, unreliable winds which are a problem for sailing ships. The Doldrums experience less severe weather than further north because the two winds are not meeting head on and are notable more for their local thunderstorms and calms than for strong and violent winds, but it is an unpredictable region.

The main circular air flow over the Atlantic Ocean around the Azores High generates the ocean currents and it is not surprising to find that these follow the same circular pattern as the winds. The big difference between the two, of course, is that while wind flow is not particularly affected by the land masses, the ocean currents are strongly influenced by contact with the continents and this can upset and divert the basic circular motion.

The north-east trade winds and their South Atlantic counterparts, the south-east trades, combine to generate a strong westward flowing current which crosses the Atlantic from Africa towards the Caribbean. This flow draws in water from both north and south along the European and African coasts. The North Equatorial Current is a strong reliable movement across the Atlantic. It hits the north coast of South America and is funnelled up into the Caribbean Sea and on into the Gulf of Mexico. Flowing at speeds of up to 3 knots the water builds up in what is virtually a cul-de-sac—the Gulf of Mexico. In the nor-thern Caribbean, with its comparatively shallow depths, the water heats up appreciably and the only way out for this warm water is through the narrow channel between Florida and Cuba. Here it flows out at a considerable speed but immediately after passing through this gap the way is blocked by the shallow seas around the Bahamas on the continental shelf of North America and the warmed water is forced to the north, parallel with the coast of the United States.

This powerful current is the famous Gulf Stream and it has a major influence on both North Atlantic and European weather. The current heads north to Cape Hatteras, at which point it is deflected out into the North Atlantic, where the flow is boosted by prevailing south-westerly winds. The Gulf Stream, or, as it becomes known, the North Atlantic Current, flows right across to Europe. The flow divides as it approaches Europe and one branch turns south to form the Portuguese Current which heads down the coast of Europe and Africa to link in once more with the North Equatorial Current, thus completing the circular flow around the ocean.

The northerly branch of the Gulf Stream continues up into the Arctic Ocean with a small branch turning back to the west just south of Iceland to form a smaller secondary circular flow in this northern part of the North Atlantic. Here it meets up with a southerly flow of cold water coming out of the Arctic and this current heads down the east coast of Greenland to meet up with another Arctic flow coming out down the west side of Greenland—the cold Labrador Current. This cold current flows across the Grand Banks of Newfoundland and down the North American coast as far as Cape Cod before it links up with the Gulf Stream and heads back in a north-easterly direction.

With the major circular flow of water around the North Atlantic, there is an area of relatively static water left in the centre. Lying at the centre of the North Atlantic circulation, the Sargasso Sea, as it is known, tends to be an area where debris, seaweed and in recent times oil slicks tend to congregate. Here large patches of Sargasso or gulf weed float on the surface. This weed often looks like low-lying land from a distance and it supports its own ecosystems. It is easy to imagine the effect of such a region on early sailors who were often sailing into unknown waters where anything different or unusual was looked on with suspicion or even dread. Since the region is also bedevilled by calms, it is easy to see why the early, highly superstitious sailors gave the Sargasso Sea a wide berth.

So much for the general circulation of the North Atlantic winds and waters, but to understand fully the effect of this circulation on the shipping of the North Atlantic, it is necessary to look at some of the more local affects of wind, weather and currents.

The Gulf Stream sweeps through the Florida Straits, between Florida and Cuba, at speeds of up to 5 knots. The straits are 50 miles wide and 350 fathoms deep creating an immense and powerful body of water. For early sailing ships this water flow must have made the Florida Straits virtually a one-way traffic system. If there was a strong wind blowing in a favourable direction to help sailing ships fight the current, then the effect of the wind working against the current would generate a very nasty short steep sea—a typical wind-against-current situation which is something to be avoided by all shipping. Even today with more efficient sailing rigs, it is a difficult passage for sail-powered vessels.

The same sort of wind-against-current seas can be found along many of the coasts bordering the northern parts of the Atlantic Ocean. Here currents in the sea are also generated by strong tides. The tides flowing in and out of the Gulf of St Lawrence, the English Channel and the North Sea twice a day, for example, generate very strong water flows. Through the Pentland Firth in the north of Scotland the tides can run at up to 9 knots quickly creating maelstrom conditions particularly when the west-going ebb tide flowing out of the North Sea meets the full force of a westerly gale sweeping in from the Atlantic. Conditions such as this can make the coastal waters on both sides of the Atlantic some of the most violent found anywhere in the world. In such seas ships can find themselves in trouble even when they have almost reached the security of harbour.

The cold Labrador Current has a lot to answer for when it comes to creating difficult sea conditions for shipping. Flowing down through the Davis Straits from the icy wastes of the Arctic it brings with it large quantities of floating ice. Much of the region through which this current flows is so cold in the winter that the sea freezes over and is a mass of solid ice, but in the early summer the ice starts to break up and melt. This 'first-year' sea ice is not too much of a hazard to navigation and most of it melts before it is carried very far south in the Labrador Current, but each summer huge sections break from the glaciers which run down from the Greenland ice cap into the Davis Strait and it is these icebergs heading south in the current which can be a major hazard.

It may take a couple of years for an iceberg to reach the Grand Banks of Newfoundland and then head even further south into the major shipping lanes. Many of these icebergs are so large that they ground on the shallow waters of the Grand Banks of Newfoundland, which stretch some 300 miles to the seaward of Newfoundland. Such huge bergs may stay grounded until they melt sufficiently to continue their southward journey over the shallow water. Eventually they are caught up by the relatively warm waters of the Gulf Stream when melting is rapid. Few icebergs reach more than 35° west before they are picked up and destroyed by the Gulf Stream, but the bergs which stay closer inshore, in the colder current, may occasionally get down as far as 40° north. Most of the icebergs which keep inshore tend to congregate just south of Cape Race on the south-east corner of Newfoundland where they eventually break up or melt.

The movement of icebergs is affected by both currents and winds and is difficult to predict. The *Titanic* disaster brought home to the public at large the risk which icebergs pose to shipping. In the days of sailing ships and in the early days of steam ships most vessels took a course directly across the Grand Banks when coming from Europe in order to make use of the Labrador Current which could help them down the coast towards the ports of Boston and New York. This took ships through the ice zone during a large part of the year but as the speed of shipping rose and the consequences of a collision with an iceberg increased there were attempts to route ocean traffic away from the ice danger. An international conference on the safety of life at sea, held in London in 1913 following the *Titanic* disaster, led to the introduction of the International Ice Patrol and although this is a service managed by the US Coast Guard, it is funded by most of the major maritime nations. The ships and aircraft of the Ice Patrol keep track of all the icebergs each season and use computer programmes to predict their future positions so warning vessels in their path. Yet ice still remains an ever-present danger, particularly when the fog often found in these latitudes reduces visibility.

Fog can be a hazard to shipping throughout much of the North Atlantic but it is particularly prevalent on the coasts of North America. Here, once again, it is the Labrador Current which is the main culprit. The meeting of the cold water of this current with the warm moist air sweeping up from the south-west creates prime conditions for fogs to form. During the summer months fog on the East Coast and out over the Grand Banks can occur as often as one day in two and the fog can stretch for hundreds of miles. In addition to hazards of fog and ice the fact that the fog is generated by a wind-against-current situation can give nasty sea conditions and it is small wonder that here is an area dreaded by seamen just as much as the Sargasso Sea. Ships coming from Europe meet this fog region just at the time when they need good visibility for a landfall and fog-reduced visibility has been responsible for many disasters in Atlantic waters. Hazards such as Sable Island off Nova Scotia and the extensive Nantucket Shoals off Cape Cod compound the navigators' problems in this region.

Bad weather and poor sea conditions are not confined to the northern part of the Atlantic. The mainly balmy waters of the Horse Latitudes are the breeding ground at certain times of the year for hurricanes—the most violent storms to be found anywhere in the world. A tropical revolving storm, to give it the official name, is similar to a depression, with the wind circulating (in the Northern Hemisphere) in an anti-clockwise direction, but here the isobars are much more concentrated than is the case with the usual anti-cyclone and the wind strength is much, much stronger. Winds of Force 7 and upwards more are unlikely more than 200 miles from the centre, but within seventy miles of the centre of the storm, gusts can exceed 150 knots, creating conditions where it is difficult to tell where the sea stops and the air begins. A hurricane is nothing short of

a seething mass of water and wind seemingly intent on destroying everything in its path. In addition its track can be highly unpredictable and its effects devastating.

For the most part tropical revolving storms occur on the western side of the northern oceans and in the Atlantic they are found generally in the West Indies and Caribbean. Here they are most frequent during the late summer and early autumn with an average of five hurricanes occurring each year. Most of the hurricanes occurring in the Atlantic start off somewhere well out to sea around latitude 20° north. The typical track of a tropical storm is to head west before turning north and then swinging out in a north-easterly direction. Thus they may head in towards the islands of the Caribbean, sometimes sweeping right in across the Gulf of Mexico or, at other times, head north up the east coast of the United States and then out into the Atlantic. Nothing is certain about the path of a hurricane, and historically their recorded tracks cover most of the western half of the Atlantic Ocean. Even when they have moderated somewhat and head up into more temperate latitudes, they are still violent storms and can continue as such right across the Atlantic and on into Europe.

Today, with aircraft and satellite coverage, hurricanes can be detected at an early stage and closely monitored, but in the past the first warning a ship might have of a hurricane approaching was a rapidly falling barometer and a darkening sky. By the time the hurricane had been detected it was probably too late to

The hazards of the North Atlantic—the Flying Enterprise *sank four days after developing a heavy list in January 1952* (Osborne collection).

escape it and the fight for survival began. Even in harbour a ship is not safe from the ravages of these violent winds and for early sailors who lacked warning systems, to be caught in one must have been worse than any nightmare.

The area known as the Bermuda Triangle falls within the hurricane region, covering much of the eastern seaboard of the United States right down to the tip of Florida. It is small wonder that it has gained a reputation for unpredictability when you consider the hurricanes which sweep the area and the very strong currents generated by the Gulf Stream. These two features in themselves are enough to generate unpredictable and violent sea conditions at short notice. Much of the Sargasso Sea also falls within the so-called 'Triangle'. Small wonder then that superstitious seamen have felt that supernatural causes lay behind some of the major disasters which have occurred in the region. Such reputations tend to be self-perpetuating, with any unexplained happening helping to further the myth.

An additional Atlantic hazard for small vessels comes from whales. In recent times, with the increase in small

The problem of wildlife—here a whale interferes with the laying of a transatlantic cable by HMS Agamemnon (Author).

craft on the ocean, there have been a number of incidents where whales have damaged or even sunk boats. The vessels used by early sailors were often little larger than many of the yachts of today and, no doubt, whales aroused their wildest fears, perhaps accounting for many of the early tales about sea monsters.

The Atlantic is indeed an inhospitable place, but it is not all bad. There are large areas with reliable and pre-dictable winds which can be of tremendous benefit to sailing ships and the wily seaman takes advantage of winds and currents in his favour. Steam-powered ships have less need to follow the dictates of the winds and currents, but they can still be friends or foes and it still pays to maintain a healthy respect for the sea. Despite its reputation for violence and unpredictable weather, man has made the North Atlantic one of the major trade routes of the world.

The early explorers

It is hard to picture a world where the huge land mass of America stretching almost from pole to pole was unknown. When Columbus set off from Spain on a westward course he was looking for China and Japan rather than any new land in between and his much heralded 'discovery' of America was almost a mistake. The West Indies were so named because the early explorers thought that they had found land somewhere in the vicinity of India and the native population of North America were called Indians for the same reason. Although Columbus is usually credited with the discovery of the American continent, however accidental, legends and rumours of its existence had existed for a long time and it is even possible that the 'lost continent of Atlantis' could have been the American continent.

I doubt that we will ever know for sure who was the true first 'discoverer' of America, but almost certainly the

Columbus sights America—a romanticized image of the landfall at San Salvador (Author).

discovery was by accident rather than by design. When you look at the current and wind circulation in the Atlantic, it is not hard to imagine a primitive boat being picked up by the north-east trade winds and the North Equatorial Current as it sailed off the coast of Africa and the crew being carried helplessly across the Atlantic. Bear in mind that early sailing vessels could make very little progress against the wind and if you combine the wind and the current running strongly to the west in this region, then there would be little hope that a boat caught up in the system would be able to make any headway back to where it started.

Such an accidental voyage across the Atlantic is credible and Columbus, on one of his later voyages, reported finding white-skinned natives in the northern regions of South America, which is the area where any boat drifting across the Atlantic would most probably have ended up. Thor Heyerdahl set out to demonstrate through his *Ra* expeditions that the ancient Egyptians could have had links with the advanced cultures found in Mexico and Peru. Heyerdahl re-enacted a possible crossing of the Atlantic in a craft constructed in the manner and style of the time and deduced from this that direct links between the two civilizations on the widely separated continents could have existed.

Heyerdahl's voyage was a courageous attempt to confirm historical theories by practical demonstration but it seems to fall down in two areas. Heyerdahl set out knowing that America existed and one must assume that the

ancient Egyptians didn't, and so it is hard to picture them setting out deliberately on such a voyage in such a craft. It is known, however, that they explored down the coast of Africa after passing through the Straits of Gibraltar and it is, perhaps, more likely that they could have been caught up in the winds and currents and made the voyage across the Atlantic by accident. This assumes that they could have survived the voyage perhaps by catching fish and drinking rain-water. Heyerdahl of course, knowing the distance involved, was able to store his boat with the appropriate requirements to make the voyage without thirst or starvation.

Even assuming that the ancient Egyptians made the trip across, there's an old saying that 'you haven't discovered something until you have told somebody else'. An astronomer, discovering a new star, simply has to let somebody have a look through his telescope to confirm the discovery. An explorer on the other hand has to make the return journey to tell people about his find and this is the worrying aspect of Heyerdahl's theory. Whilst it is comparatively easy to accept that a papyrus boat could have crossed the Atlantic from east to west, and Heyerdahl demonstrated that this was possible, it is much harder to visualize the same craft making the return journey. The only feasible route would have been to pick up the Gulf Stream and make the long journey north-about, and that really doesn't seem to be a possibility in such a craft and with a crew totally ignorant of currents and navigation. If the arrival in the New World was accidental then it is hard to picture such an advanced civilization as existed in Mexico or Peru being developed from a few shipwrecked sailors. We will never know for sure the origins of these civilizations, but I think that we can reasonably assume that the first early voyages across the Atlantic were made from east to west and by accident.

One of the first records of purposeful voyages of discovery out on the Atlantic is found in the voyages of St Brendan. There were claims that around 570 AD, St Brendan crossed the Atlantic to America and in the manner of Thor Heyerdahl a reconstruction of such a voyage was carried out by Tim Severin in 1976-7 in a replica craft. The general consensus, however, is that St Brendan managed to reach the southern shores of Iceland and also sailed southwards to the Azores, but that he didn't make it the whole way across the Atlantic. This is not to detract from what were certainly brave voyages of discovery in a fragile craft and it was nearly 400 years later before the Vikings made what is now generally taken to be the first European landing on the American continent and this was certainly a result of a navigational error rather than a planned voyage of discovery.

By the year 900 AD the Vikings had moved out across the oceans to Iceland and Greenland and gained much experience of sailing on these inhospitable northern waters. This far north, the currents, if not directly in their favour, were at least not against them. Capable of being propelled by oars as

well as sails, the Viking ships were not entirely reliant on favourable winds. It is speculated that the first sighting of the North American continent by Bjarni Herjulfsson came about because he steered the wrong course or was diverted from his course by unusual winds and not because he had any exploratory motives. Herjulfsson had set out from Iceland to make the trip to the newly-established colonies on Greenland and the Viking sagas record that he landed in a strange land. Later researchers have suggested that this first landing point was in the Cape Cod area. In terms of the prevailing winds and currents, this seems an unlikely landfall for somebody making for Greenland, even taking into account the rudimentary navigation techniques of the time. Although strong currents run down both sides of Greenland which could have taken the boat to the south and made it miss Greenland altogether, the most likely landfall then would be in the region of Newfoundland or Labrador—assuming that the boat was steering a reasonably consistent heading.

Herjulfsson apparently didn't take the trouble to explore the new lands, but rather was intent on getting back to Greenland, and Leif Erikson has the claim to being the first European to set foot on American soil. This was some seventeen years after Herjulfsson had made his discovery and Erikson's voyage to America may have been for a purpose as mundane as collecting wood for the Viking colony on Greenland. Erikson actually established a colony on the new continent, although its exact location has never been clearly identified. This was a seasonal colony and for several years thereafter the Greenland Vikings visited the area to collect timber. Thus this so-called 'first discovery' of America was a fairly casual affair and the significance of the discovery was not really appreciated. However, the word 'discovery' is correct because both boats and crews returned to tell the story.

These first two crossings of the Atlantic followed the most practical routes for low-powered vessels which would have difficulty sailing against the wind. While the southern route was long but favoured by consistent winds and currents, the northerly route across the Atlantic allowed a degree of island hopping which was a help with basic navigation techniques and had reasonably favourable currents. The northern route is also prone to storms and cold which must have made the Viking voyages pretty daunting affairs. These early

sailors had no knowledge of ocean currents or wind patterns. Their navigation skills too were pretty basic, since they lacked compasses, but it has been suggested that they could work out latitudes from the sun and stars. In the circumstances it is quite easy to see why Herjulfsson raised the American coast rather than Greenland and it is a tribute to his navigation skills that he was able to find his way back to Greenland. The reduced distances involved in the northern island-hopping route would have helped.

The voyages of Columbus across the Atlantic were even more daring and courageous because he set out into the unknown with a very well-defined purpose—namely to find Japan by going 'the wrong way round the world'. Columbus has gone down in history as a famous explorer with good cause, but it should be remembered that at the time he set out westwards, the Azores had

A replica Viking ship, similar in size to those used to make the first recorded Atlantic crossings.

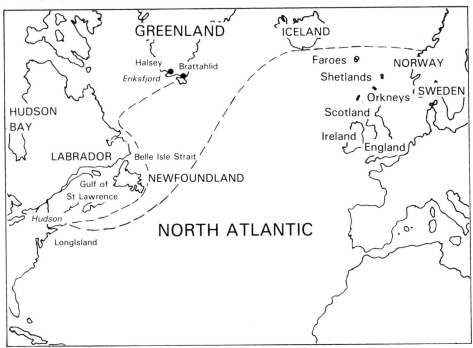

A map showing the route possibly taken by Bjarni Herjulfson when he landed on American soil, although the chances are that he did not get as far south as Cape Cod.

already been discovered and, since they lie some 700 miles to the west of Spain, it is clear that ships were already ranging well out into the Atlantic. The Canary Islands to the south were also well known and these were the first stopping off point for Columbus on his voyage of discovery.

Columbus took a fleet of three ships. This was a sensible precaution because on a voyage into the unknown there was an obvious risk of losing ships through storm or through grounding: three ships increased the likelihood that one or two would survive the voyage. In the light of present day shipping experience, the vessels which Columbus took were remarkably small, being little bigger than many of the yachts which sail the Atlantic today. The flagship of the little fleet, the *Santa Maria*, ranks as one of the most famous ships in history, but in fact few details have survived. Her overall length is believed to have been around 85 ft and when you consider that this includes the bowsprit, the hull itself was probably no more than 70 ft in length. The other two vessels taken by Columbus, the *Pinta* and the *Nina*, were even smaller, probably under 60 ft in length, but as Columbus says in his account of the voyage, 'smaller ships are desirable on voyages of discovery because of their handiness when sailing in strange and uncharted waters'.

Once Columbus left the Canary Islands, he headed on a course which was almost due west. Navigation techniques were still elementary but the elevation of the Pole Star above the horizon enabled navigators to maintain a fairly consistent latitude: indeed, the starting point of the Canary Islands and the landing point at San Salvador are on almost the same latitude. Columbus set out with the intention of finding Japan and since the southern islands of Japan are only slightly further north in latitude than the Canary Islands, he was on the right track—although he was a few thousand miles out in his calculation of longitude!

What must have been most worrying for Columbus on his outward voyage across was the constant presence of favourable winds. Favourable winds are fine if you want to get somewhere quickly, but there must have been the nagging doubt that it might be necessary to find the way back against these same consistent breezes. Columbus would not have known about the currents which were also helping him and against which he would also have to battle on his return journey.

On his arrival in what became known as the West Indies, Columbus spent some time exploring amongst the islands but his crews were getting restless and the *Pinta* deserted the expedition to sail back for Europe. Later the *Santa Maria* was lost after being wrecked on a sandbank at an anchorage and this left Columbus with only the diminutive *Nina* to make the voyage back to Spain. After establishing a settlement, the re-maining members of the expedition set off in the *Nina* heading on a north-easterly track which represented the best course that could be maintained in the prevailing wind conditions. On this northerly route both the *Nina* and the *Pinta* ahead of it experienced tremendous seas, perhaps encountering a hurricane, such a frequent phenomenon in the region.

The *Nina* overtook the *Pinta* on the return journey, enabling Columbus to arrive back in Spain first with the news of his discovery. It was an epic voyage into the unknown but perhaps most significant for future exploration was the fact that Columbus returned with gold artefacts. Even though he hadn't discovered the riches of the east, there was sufficient promise of riches from the new lands to whet the appetite for further voyages. Columbus himself made three more voyages to the New World, the first of these with seventeen ships and 1,500 men. On this major expedition he discovered many of the islands comprising the West Indies and on his third voyage he found the mainland of South America where he came across the white-faced natives.

Columbus has gone down in history as the discoverer of America, but the reality is that both he and many subsequent explorers, when they realized that these new lands were not the Chinese or Japanese coastline that they were seeking, spent much of their time trying to find a way round or through the huge American continent to get to the Far East. News of the voyages of Columbus spread, and from Britain John Cabot set out in the *Matthew*, a small three-masted trading vessel about 65 ft in length, to find some of the fabled riches for Britain. Cabot set out from Bristol in 1497 and after little more than a month on the Atlantic sighted either Newfoundland or Cape Breton Island. For an east-west passage across the North Atlantic, this voyage by Cabot was remarkably quick: he probably took a fairly northerly route and was favoured by winds and currents. While this may have been more by accident than design, there is some evidence that the fisheries of the Grand Banks area were already being exploited by British vessels. Indeed one is led to the conclusion that the expeditions which led to recorded landfalls on the coasts of America were probably preceded by many earlier wide-ranging voyages. It is more than likely that land had been sighted on such earlier journeys. While these sightings have not been recorded for posterity, they may have encouraged early explorers to embark on deliberate voyages of discovery.

Like Columbus, Cabot, after his first expedition to North America with (in his case) but a single ship, managed to get a lot more support for a second expedition and he set off the following year with a fleet of six vessels. Atlantic storms, however, seem to have caught up with the fleet and little is known about their fate except that one put into an Irish port.

The significant aspect of Cabot's voyage was not so much the rediscovery of mainland North America after the Viking voyages many years before, but the establishment of the Grand Banks fisheries. By the year 1500 fleets from many of the south-western British ports ventured out across the Atlantic to fish in these prolific waters. Only eight years after Columbus made his historic voyage, small fishing boats were making the arduous trip across the Atlantic with the prosaic motive of catching fish rather than glamorous ideas about discovering new lands. History has endowed many of the early discoverers with high and pure motives for their voyages into the unknown, but in all probability the motives were essentially those of greed and personal gain: the prospect of finding untold wealth was always a powerful motivating force.

For the Spaniards, who continued to explore and exploit the lands around the Caribbean Sea, wealth was found amongst the riches of the Inca and the Aztec civilizations and between 1500 and 1600 Spanish ships made regular voyages taking countless settlers across to establish colonies in the new lands and returning to Spain laden with treasure. It is small wonder that the British and the French cast envious eyes at these Spanish treasure ships and it was not long before what amounted to piracy on the high seas was under way as these nations attacked returning Spanish ships in order to get a share of the riches of the new territories.

By the early 16th century the Atlantic was being crossed regularly, but the ships involved were still very small and history tends to record the successful voyages rather than the ones which didn't make it. These small and, by present day standards, very primitive vessels must have been extremely tough

A sailing ship of around 1630. This vessel has a length of just over 100 ft and was armed with 23 guns despite being primarily a cargo vessel.

on their crews and, in the North Atlantic, storms must have taken a heavy toll. Even in the better conditions on the sailing route which followed the North Equatorial Current, the Spanish ships and later their attackers from northern Europe must have experienced hurricanes and other navigational hazards. Sailing the Atlantic remained a venture into the unknown and for the superstitious sailor the long days at sea without sighting land, the bad weather, basic food and very limited water must have created conditions where death was a constant companion.

The lure of new lands and new riches, however, maintained a high level of exploration. In 1534 the French explorer Jacques Cartier was the first to sail up the St Lawrence River. Like many early explorers, Cartier was looking for a way around the American continent and was rather less interested in exploring it. Although he is credited with the 'exploration' of this part of North America, European fishing vessels were already using the lower reaches of the river for shelter and indeed on Cartier's first voyage a French fishing schooner dropped anchor close by in the mouth of the St Lawrence.

Even before Cartier's journey, the French ship *Dauphine*, commanded by an Italian, Giovanni Da Verrazano, had explored much of the continental coastline further north and discovered what is now New York harbor, where his name is perpetuated in the bridge across the narrows at the entrance. Verrazano was one of the first to realize that the American continent was not in fact the Far East, although many years would elapse before it was appreciated that America was cut off from Asia entirely.

Increasing trade across the Atlantic and further voyages of exploration led to the development of larger ships. When ships had been following coastal routes, the need was for smaller handy ships to cope with the difficult coastal conditions, but for ocean travel the need for larger ships was increasingly recognized. Expanded maritime trade routes and the associated national wealth and prestige which went with them increased the importance of naval power and led to the development of such warships as the *Henry Grace à Dieu* in England and in France, *Grand François*. In Sweden, a large warship 174 ft long and with a beam of 40 ft was named, appropriately, the *Elefant*. The technology developed in the construction of these flagships of the fleet spilled over into the design of merchant vessels which also continued to increase in size. Increasingly too, trading vessels were required to be heavily armed for defence against the ships of other nations sailing on Atlantic waters. By the mid 16th century ships with a length between 100 ft and 120 ft were regularly used for trans-ocean voyages. They were also being built to more seaworthy forms with much more attention being paid to rigs which were strong and divided up into smaller sails for easy handling in bad weather conditions. Three and four-masted vessels became common but sailing with the wind anywhere forward of the beam remained a problem.

For their size, all of these ships carried enormous crews and life on board must have been miserable in the extreme, particularly in cold northern waters. There would be no heating on board except for the galley fire—and that would normally be on deck and have to be put out in bad weather. Hot food would not be available when it was needed most. With all the other risks of sailing in unchartered waters it is small wonder that mutiny was never far away. The popular and romantic picture of seamen ready to fight for king and country was a long way from the reality of the very primitive conditions which existed on board. For the Captains there was the prospect of making a fortune out of a successful voyage and this was the incentive which made the risks and hardship worthwhile.

With the the increasing number of ships making the Atlantic crossing during the 16th century, an understanding of wind and current patterns developed steadily. Navigation was still more an art than a science and no means of measuring longitude had been developed other than by checking the distance travelled. With the introduction of the astrolabe, latitude could be determined with reasonable accuracy and ships gained basic compasses to give them an idea of direction. A pattern of voyages developed in which ships would leave Europe and head south with favourable winds and currents to the coast of Africa where they would pick up the North Equatorial Current and the north-east trades to make the Atlantic crossing to the west. Returning, the ships would pick up the Gulf Stream and the prevailing south-westerlies to make the trip back to Europe across a more northerly track and thus a circular pattern of trade developed, a pattern which was to persist throughout the history of the sailing ship on the Atlantic. Even today modern yachts with their adequate windward capability still tend to follow this basic Atlantic routing.

Since navigators could measure only latitude with a reasonable degree of accuracy, ships tended to follow due east or west courses across the Atlantic,

The Lloyd, *typical of the trading ships of the eighteenth century, small handy vessels of 100-120 ft in length* (Bristol City Archives).

maintaining a steady latitude until they found land which would give them an indication of their longitude. Once the landfall had been made they would then either follow the coast 'up' or 'down' to the latitude of their destination, or alternatively head due north (or south) until they hit this latitude, and then head east or west as appropriate. These courses assumed that the winds would allow them to sail in the desired direction and in many cases prolonged storms could blow the ship a long way off course. It is small wonder that shipping casualties were frequent in the 16th century particularly as vessels were making their landfall.

One of the biggest problems facing shipping was the inability of the sailing ship to make progress to windward. Almost inevitably when the vessel was approaching land it would be approaching with the wind from somewhere abaft the beam and there was always the risk of the vessel becoming embayed and unable to beat out to windward to escape from the clutches of the land. The American coastline was probably not as dangerous in this respect as the European coastline where the Bay of Biscay became much feared by seamen heading home. Ships were often trapped in the bay by the prevailing westerly winds and found themselves driven remorselessly towards, and eventually against, the shore, unable to beat to windward and clear the ensnaring arms of the coastline.

By the mid 16th century, when Magellan had shown that the world was round by sailing round Cape Horn and out into the Pacific, the broad exploration of the American coastline was largely complete and numerous settlements existed in the New World. In the south the Spaniards established their superiority over the local population with strong demonstrations of force, but the northern colonists on mainland America had a much more difficult time with the aggressive native Indians. Gradually, however, the colonies were established and voyages of discovery across the Atlantic became increasingly voyages of trade or piracy.

In the second half of the 16th century the British became particularly bold on Atlantic and Caribbean waters. These were the days of Hawkins, Drake, Frobisher and Howard who set out with official sanction to attack Spanish shipping. It was John Hawkins who effectively began the slave trade across the Atlantic. Sailing out from England he would head south down the coast of Africa to pick up slaves on the African coast and then take the favourable current across the Atlantic to the West Indies and to the Americas where surviving slaves could be sold off. After attacking Spanish galleons and loading up with treasure from this source, he

would take the favourable Gulf Stream to make a quick passage back to Europe. This triangular trade pattern was to be followed for the next century and a half although more latterly ships would load up with legitimate cargoes of tobacco or cotton from the New World for sale in the markets of Europe, instead of plundered Spanish goods.

The first passenger services across the Atlantic, if they can be called such, involved the shipping of parties of colonists to found settlements in North America. Later came the slave trade where the 'passengers' were certainly unwilling travellers. On these early 'passenger' trips the conditions must have been absolutely appalling. Bad as the conditions were for sailors on the Atlantic, for the passengers the conditions were even worse and they were often battened down below for days on end when weather conditions were bad. Food and water would be restricted and poor in condition to the extent that scurvy was a major problem amongst seafarers and passengers alike on long ocean crossings. Privation and disease were the rule rather than the exception on both slavers and ships carrying colonists.

By 1600 British ships were firmly established on the Atlantic, and the Spanish influence was starting to wane. But now there was another seafaring nation and the Dutch, after a late start, were beginning to make their mark on the naval scene. By 1630 they had seized a number of West Indian islands from the Spaniards and were established in New Amsterdam, later to become New

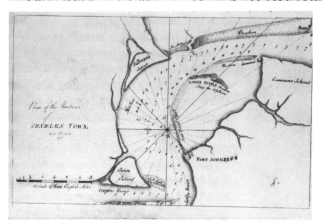

Above *Log extract from the* Lloyd *which crossed the Atlantic in 1772 and 1774. Note that only the latitude is given but longitude is compared with the estimate of a passing ship* (Bristol City Archives).

Left *The basic charts of the eighteenth century. This is Charlestown in 1767* (Bristol City Archives).

couple of rowing boats, as often as not totally inadequate for the number of people on board, especially when colonists were being carried. In any case the chances of survival from a ship which was in distress were low. The best that could be hoped for was that a passing ship would see their plight. With the increasing traffic on the Atlantic, this chance was increasing, but shipping casualties remained high, with up to one in five vessels being lost each year. Only the large profits which could accrue from successful voyages encouraged shipowners to continue to send their ships across the Atlantic. Throughout the history of Atlantic travel the profit motive has justified the risks involved but the cost, in terms of human life, must have been considerable.

The rise and fall of the Atlantic sailing packet

At the end of the 18th century and the beginning of the 19th century were periods of considerable political turmoil on both sides of the Atlantic. In America the colonists were coming to terms with their new found independence, whilst further north Britain had taken over Canada from the French and so retained territorial rights over at least part of the continent. In the south the Spaniards were retreating from territories in Central and South America and in the Caribbean the British and the French were still in hot competition for the various islands. In Europe the French Revolution was underway and Napoleon made his bid for power. The Battle of Trafalgar took place in 1805 but it was 1815 before the Battle of Waterloo restored peace to the European scene, and commerce across the Atlantic could resume a more normal pattern.

Over the three previous centuries since Columbus sailed across the Atlantic commerce had developed into a regular although still very risky business. Trading ships were small, rarely exceeding 180 ft in length and the achievement lay in completing a passage rather than in making fast passages or establishing records. Ships were sailed with comparatively small crews and the life expectancy of both ship and crew was short.

Despite the political upheaval trade across the Atlantic continued. By 1800 it was very much a two-way operation with manufactured goods and luxuries being taken out from Europe and the ships returning loaded with tobacco and cotton and sugar from the south, and timber, fish products and firs from the northern regions of the new continent. The timber trade is particularly significant because it demonstrates the shortage of timber which was being found in Europe, particularly timber suitable for shipbuilding. This shortage of timber was a major factor behind the move by European yards to build the first composite ships—with iron framing and wooden planking — and then ships built completely of iron.

On the American side of the Atlantic there was timber to be had for the taking from the vast forests and a large export trade developed. Shipyards were established to take advantage of the timber reserves and these yards were eventually to produce some of the most magnificent sailing ships ever seen on

Atlantic waters. Even as early as 1700 North American yards were building roughly half of the sailing ships which were trading across the Atlantic and towards the end of the 18th century nearly a third of British-*owned* ships were built in North America, to take advantage of the lower costs of raw materials. Most of the new timber was of the softwood variety and the ships were built with new techniques to match the material being used.

At this time European warships were being built in the magnificent three and four-deck style typified by HMS *Victory*, best known as Nelson's flagship. These warships were a throwback to the vessels of the Spanish Armada where firing power from the cannons was considered more important than speed and manoeuvrability. On the other side of the Atlantic a much handier faster type of warship was being developed and epitomized by the frigates *United States* and *Constitution* which were both launched in 1797. When the fighting in the War of Independence ceased, the shipbuilders again turned their attention to the requirements of trade. The North American shipyards developed the famous schooners which both served the fisheries on the Grand Banks of Newfoundland and carried dried fish to the markets of Europe. These schooners were equally handy and fast, small vessels which could make rapid passages

to and from the fishing grounds and across the Atlantic. Although equipped with fore and aft sails to give them a much better ability to make progress to windward, it was their fine underwater lines which gave them their speed and which served as prototypes for the great tradition of the American clipper ships and the speed they brought to the crossing of the Atlantic under sail.

Attention invariably tends to be focussed on the fast vessels even though they are a small minority of the vessels plying Atlantic waters. The vast majority of vessels trading on the Atlantic at the beginning of the 19th century were full bodied, comparatively slow and unwieldy craft with the accent on carrying capacity rather than elegance and speed. Trading vessels remained at risk from attack by the ships of unfriendly nations and convoy systems were used to give mutual protection. Even then other factors could still bring about disaster. One such convoy set out from Cork in 1804 with 69 merchant ships and two warships bound for the West Indies and headed south to pick up the favourable winds and currents: 29 of the ships in this convoy subsequently ran aground, with heavy loss of life, on the coast of Portugal. This disaster demonstrates that determining longitude with accuracy continued to be a problem even when a whole convoy of ships was involved. The chronometer, deemed successful in 1773 for determining longitude, did not come into universal use for nearly a century thereafter.

The more settled situation in North America after the War of Independence

---

Left *HMS* St Vincent *was built in 1810 when sailing warships were reaching the peak of their development. She carries 120 guns* (Author).

Above *The loss of the emigrant ship* Tayleur *on the Irish coast in 1854: 300 lives were lost in this incident* (Liverpool Maritime Museum).

Right *An emigrant ship loading at Liverpool just before departing for the New World* (Illustrated London News).

and the vast tracts of land available for colonization, was in stark contrast to the crowded cities of Europe and the starvation levels of subsistence in parts of the European countryside. The earlier colonists gave way to a rising tide of emigrants across the Atlantic which was to be a feature of Atlantic shipping for the next hundred years. The emigrant trade took in people from most European countries but built up slowly at first. However by 1850 over a million emigrants a year were making the passage across the Atlantic. This new emigrant trade brought increased business for the shipowners and formed what was probably the first real passenger-carrying service across the Atlantic, although accommodation still left much to be desired. Emigrant ships were usually converted cargo ships with temporary accommodation built below decks for the passengers. On the return journey the ships would revert to their cargo-carrying role and be loaded with timber or other produce for the passage back across the Atlantic. When functioning as emigrant ships accommodation would be basic with two or three tiers of bunks knocked up from rough hewn timber. Space was at a premium because the more emigrants carried, the more the shipowner got paid: in crowded conditions emigrants would be packed as tightly as the shipowners dared and cooking and toilet facilities would be as primitive as owners thought they could get away with.

Seasickness must have been a major problem with the emigrants battened down below decks in anything but the finest of weather. Deaths on the crossing were a common occurrence and as the fare had to be paid before boarding there was little incentive for the shipowners to improve conditions to ensure that their 'passengers' survived. Thus the emigrant trade was in direct contrast to the slave trade where the shipowner had every incentive to keep his human

cargo in good condition so that they could be sold on arrival. With the emigrants there was no such motive and epidemics of cholera and other infectious diseases were quite common on board. Up to a quarter of the emigrants might die on a passage across the Atlantic but there was also a lively birth rate on board these vessels so that on occasion the number of emigrants on arrival might exceed that of departure!

The emigrant trade was so lucrative for shipowners that all sorts of vessels were pressed into service to take advantage of the trade. One record reports that the sailing ship *Vestal* which sailed from Scotland to Prince Edward Island in Canada arrived with 301 'passengers' although she was only 90 ft in length. Even smaller was the *Peter And Sarah* which took emigrants to Prince Edward Island in 1818: she was only 50 ft in length. It is small wonder then, that around 16 per cent of all those who emigrated to Canada in 1847 died either on the passage or shortly after arrival and these figures are by no means unusual.

One of the big problems with the emigrant trade was the time taken for the westward passage: for many ships, particularly the smaller ones, a passage of fifty or sixty days was considered quite normal. Battling for week after week against winds and currents was inevitable unless they took the option of the cold route to the north or the much longer but warmer route to the south, and neither of these was likely to improve the health of the emigrants. That the trade continued in the way it did says

much for the life the new arrivals found and a lot about the conditions they left behind. Perhaps they kept to a minimum their reports about the journey in letters and news back to other potential emigrants. Since few could write anyway, perhaps new travellers set off in blissful ignorance, buoyed up by the hopes and promises of the 'promised land' on the other side. Emigrant ships sailed summer and winter for the New World and shipwreck, fire and storms took their toll of the human cargoes. The barque *John* ran aground on rocks shortly after leaving Plymouth in 1855 and the master and crew abandoned the ship leaving the emigrants on board to their fate, with many of them drowning as the ship broke up. This is just one example of the hundreds of vessels which suffered severe damage or were totally wrecked on their passage across the stormy Atlantic. Emigrants took their chance between the conflicting perils of shipwreck and disease. With the absence of safety regulations and equipment, it is perhaps remarkable that enough survived the passage to populate the vast new continents across the ocean.

In 1820 more than 1,000 journeys were made across the Atlantic with timber cargoes for the British Isles. Twenty years later that number had more than doubled. With a ship making perhaps only two return passages a year this figure for 1840 equates to 1,000 ships and to this must be added a similar number of ships bringing cotton and other goods from America. This was only the trade to the British Isles and in total there were probably 5,000 or more

Facilities on sailing ships remained primitive for many years: steering a ship in a heavy Atlantic sea exposed the helmsman to the weather.

ships regularly sailing on the Atlantic routes by the mid 1820s. One-way trade is rarely profitable but here they could carry traditional produce one way and return westwards with a human cargo, to such a profitable extent that as the emigrant trade increased the fares charged actually dropped so that by 1840 an emigrant would be charged perhaps only £3 for the Atlantic passage (a figure equivalent to a seaman's wages for a month and a half). The American Civil War in 1861 brought a temporary halt to the emigrant trade and also introduced other restrictions to commercial activity, but by this date the governments on both sides of the Atlantic had in any case started to regulate the emigrant trade, calling for minimum standards and conditions on board ships. The steamship was also entering service and conditions on board these ships were a vast improvement over those found on sailing vessels. The promise of a regular and predictable passage across the Atlantic provided compe-

tition which the sailing ships could not match. As far as the sailing ships were concerned, the emigrant trade was coming to an end by 1860. From this point on the significance of the trade carried by sailing ships across the Atlantic started to diminish, although their finest hour was still to come.

Not all the passenger movement across the Atlantic was migrant traffic. With the industrial revolution taking place firstly in Europe and then in North America, there was an increasing demand from people with adequate means for a comfortable passage across the ocean. Emigrants who had made money wanted to return to see relatives in Europe and the demand for regular passenger trade in both directions across the Atlantic started to grow. Passengers on sailing ships who could afford it would pay for a cabin located aft amongst the officers' quarters on the ship. On most sailing ships there was little provision made for carrying passengers in this way and it would be rare to find cabin accommodation for more than ten passengers. Gradually, the demands for regular passenger services and the rapid transport of sensitive cargoes led to the development of the packet ship. This new concept in ocean transportation put an emphasis on speed and reliability with sailing schedules being advertised and proper provision being made for passenger carrying. Ships were built for speed and in the passages of these packet ships we start getting references to fast crossings and record journey times for the first time.

The first record of an advertised sailing for a sailing ship carrying passengers dates from 1817 and announces that the 424-ton *James Monroe* would sail from New York to Liverpool on 5 January 1818. The same advertisement said that the *Couvier* would sail from Liverpool on 1 January for New York and that regular monthly sailings would continue. So began the era of regular advertised shipping services and the establishment of the famous Black Ball Line, setting the stage for the quest for speed across the Atlantic. Now there was no longer any achievement in just making the passage across the Atlantic. These scheduled passenger services were made possible by the use of ships designed with a hull form to give maximum speed and a rig which would enable them to make progress in light breezes and yet sufficiently strong to enable large areas of canvas to be carried in strong winds. Driving these large and powerful sailing ships was a new breed of men, tough, ruthless, but above all excellent seamen who would push their ships to the limit in

order to make fast passages.

The dividing line between driving a ship to its reasonable limits and recklessness is a narrow one and the reputations for fast Atlantic crossings were made by those Captains who could keep just on the right side of this line. The successful Captains who established the records were treated like gods, both feared and respected by seamen, but their reputations were only as good as their last passage. The North Atlantic is no respecter of reputation and their determination could prove their undoing should they take one chance too many and push their ships to the point where things started to break.

The packet ships, or 'clipper ships' as they became known in some trades, were largely an American development. They had their origins in the shipyards on the East Coast of North America, and were generally larger than their predecessors. Average ship lengths rose from around 160 ft to 200 ft or more. The largest of the clipper ships was 250 ft in length, still a small ship by comparison with ships we know today, but for ships built in wood and carrying vast areas of sail these vessels marked the peak of the shipbuilders' art. For European owners the prospect of building a ship in North America offered numerous advantages, not least an initially attractive price and the ability to immediately pick up a timber cargo for the maiden voyage eastwards across the Atlantic.

At the beginning of the 19th century two Scottish naval architects and shipbuilders, John and Charles Wood (appropriately enough), took this prac-

Sail handling on a square rigger was a hazardous occupation (American Merchant Marine Academy).

tice to a logical extreme to avoid a tax on imported timber brought into Britain, conceiving the idea of importing timber into Britain by constructing a solid ship of timber, sailing her across the Atlantic with a full cargo and breaking her up for the timber in her frames on arrival. This ship was to be designed specifically for the purpose and to be built as cheaply as possible in order to allow as much of the squared timber to be re-used once it had been brought to Britain. The fact that this timber was actually part of a ship meant that it wouldn't be regarded as being imported as cargo and could thus evade the tax.

John and Charles Wood were not inexperienced: they had designed and built the steamboat *Comet* way back in 1812. They travelled to Canada to build the *Columbus* and the *Baron of Renfrew*; the former, built in 1824, had a length of 301 ft and a beam of 50 ft, making her, in all

likelihood, the largest ship of her day. Packed with solid timber and rigged as a four-masted barque, the *Columbus* was towed down the St Lawrence but went aground and much of the timber had to be jettisoned to refloat her. The *Columbus* made the voyage across the Atlantic safely although it was reported that there was 18 ft of water in her hold on arrival in London. The timber cargo was discharged from the ship, but rather than break her up her greedy owners decided to send her back for another cargo and on this return voyage she foundered—you can't take chances with the Atlantic.

The *Baron of Renfrew* was slightly larger at 304 ft long and with a beam of 61 ft. Launched in 1825 she too successfully crossed the Atlantic on her maiden voyage, but went aground in the Thames estuary and eventually drifted onto the French coast where she broke up. In terms of size the *Columbus* and the *Baron of Renfrew* were well ahead of their time and it was thirty years before their size was eclipsed by the clipper ship *Great Republic*, designed and built by the famous Donald McKay at Boston. The *Great Republic* as originally constructed had a length of 335 ft and a 53 ft beam and went on to make one of the fastest-ever sailing ship crossings of the Atlantic in 1855.

As mentioned earlier, the first packet line to be established was the Black Ball Line, which began operations with the *James Monroe, Couvier, Amity* and *Pacific* in 1818. These vessels made regular sailings, had comfortable cabin layouts and were specifically designed for passenger operation—cargo carrying being very much a secondary consideration in their design. Although only a maximum of 500 tons, each ship was equipped with a large dining room, 40 ft by 14 ft, panelled in mahogany and satinwood, with seven passenger state rooms off each side. The success of their operation may be judged by the fact that after six months in service, four more ships were added to the fleet with sailings now advertised on the first and sixteenth of each month: a year later the fleet was expanded with four more vessels. During the first years of the Black Ball Line's existence the average eastbound crossing took 23 days and the westbound crossing forty days. The *Canada*, one of the later ships to be added to the fleet, set a record for the best crossing from New York to Liverpool in 15 days and 18 hours in 1823.

The Captains of these and other packet ships were expected to drive them extremely hard and such was the pressure on the hull and rigging that few vessels lasted more than a few years in this demanding service. However, the Black Ball Line prospered in its endeavours and as the packet trade developed the ships rapidly increased in size from the initial 500 tons up to 1,500 tons. One of the fastest ships on the Atlantic in 1852 was the *Fidelia*, of just under 1,000 tons, which made a record run from New York to the North West Lightship off Liverpool in 13 days 7 hours—and a remarkably fast run on a westbound passage of 17 days 6 hours. The *Fidelia* was built by William H. Webb of New York who, along with Donald McKay, was responsible for many of the fast and famous large sailing ships built in America.

Competition was not far behind as the speed of the passage became the critical factor in the minds of the passengers. The success of the Black Ball Line led to the establishment of other packet ship companies: the Red Star Line was founded in 1821 and the Swallow Tail Line the following year. The Red Star Line had sailings on the 24th of every month from New York while the Swallow Tail Line sailed on the 8th, thus dovetailing their services comfortably into those of the Black Ball Line to give weekly crossings on the Atlantic route. All these early services went into Liverpool but later the Swallow Tail Line established services direct to London, this service being operated by four ships of only 400 tons. The Black X Line was also established in the 1820s to operate the service between New York and London and used similar small ships but later went on to build more luxurious vessels such as the 1,000 ton *Victoria*, which created a sensation with its luxurious accommodation.

The Dramatic Line was established in the late 1830s by Captain E. K. Collins who later gave his name to the Collins Line steamships. Like the other vessels operating these Atlantic passenger packet services the Dramatic Line ships were typically 180 ft in length with a beam of 36 ft, small ships by present day standards but extremely toughly built. Despite the luxurious appointments a crossing must still have been quite an experience even for the first class passengers. Driving a sailing ship hard would give it a very uncomfortable motion and no matter how much effort was put into creating a luxurious environment, the risks of a sailing ship crossing of the Atlantic, particularly in winter, could not be entirely disguised.

On the journey from England to New York the packet ships continued to carry emigrants in the holds but still reserved accommodation for first class passengers. Gradually as the passenger trade developed, a second class passenger division was also introduced thus setting the pattern for three classes of Atlantic passengers which was to be followed later by the steamships.

Competition between the shipping lines soon became intense and by the mid 1830s there were forty or more ships sailing between North America and Europe on scheduled sailings. As rivalry increased it was inevitable that sailings would be made on the same day by different lines and thus develop into races across the Atlantic. One of the first of these races took place between the *Columbus*, (not to be confused with the Canadian-built timber ship *Columbus*), the *George Washington* and the *Sheffield*. These three ships left New York on the same day, but the *George Washington* was the first to be sighted off Holyhead three hours in front of the *Sheffield*, having made the crossing in seventeen days. Although the *Columbus* was the loser in this 1836 race, she challenged the Dramatic liner *Sheridan* to a race across the Atlantic for a stake of $20,000. On this occasion the *Columbus* made the crossing in sixteen days with the *Sheridan* over two days later. This was the maiden voyage of the *Sheridan* so perhaps she may be excused for not being in full racing trim.

Despite the advertised reliability of the service, at least as far as departures were concerned, events often dictated otherwise, particularly on the passage westbound from England to America. The packet *Hendrick Hudson* took seventy days for one crossing and then foundered on a later westbound crossing when she was carrying a cargo of iron rails. Even if the total loss of a packet ship was fortunately rare, damage to spars and rigging was frequent, particularly when these vessels were driven hard. Owners, however, accepted rigging failures as part of the price they had to pay for fast crossings, even on the most well-constructed ship.

Public interest in fast crossings was

sustained and fostered by the shipping companies since their popularity, and hence profits, largely depended on their reputation for speed and reliability. Sailing packet services were soon being offered from ports other than New York on the American coast with Boston and Philadelphia being important terminals for transatlantic sailings. On the European side, Liverpool remained the main port for the packet ships but London, the French port of Le Havre and some of the German ports soon entered the fray. On the main routes the size of ship continued to increase as did the speed of the crossings. Sixteen days was quite a commonplace time for the Atlantic crossing on the eastbound trip by the 1850s. On the westbound trip, the packet ship *Emerald* made a very rapid passage in seventeen days from Liverpool to Boston as early as 1824 but anything under three weeks could be considered a fast passage against the prevailing winds and currents.

Brown and Bell built all the early Dramatic Line ships and later the *Patrick Henry*, a 1,000-ton ship which made an Atlantic crossing in fourteen days. By 1846, however, their reputation was being challenged by the famous Donald McKay concern. One of the first vessels built at this yard was the *New World* which, at 1,400 tons, was one of the largest of the packet ships of the mid 1800s. Shipbuilder Donald McKay had firm ideas about design and was responsible for many improvements in the size, speed and performance of the packet ships. Born in Nova Scotia, he moved south to New York and by thirty years of age he was at the top of the ship designing and building profession. By the age of 34 he had set up his own shipbuilding yard at Boston which was to produce many famous packet and clipper ships. The *Staffordshire*, of 1,817 tons, was built in 1851, and in 1853 the yard went on to build the *Star of Empire* and the *Chariot of Fame* which were the largest packet ships ever built at 2,050 tons. None of these vessels broke any records on the Atlantic, but they set the pattern for the clipper ships for which McKay was to become famous.

American and Canadian shipyards

were the birthplace of the clipper ship. These vessels were primarily designed for operating over the long distance routes from Europe and USA to Australia, and from the East Coast of the USA round the Horn to the gold prospecting areas of the West Coast. By 1850, steam was starting to take over the comparatively short Atlantic passenger routes but could not yet compete on the long distance routes because of the need for frequent coaling. Nevertheless many clipper ships although designed primarily for other routes made Atlantic crossings on their maiden voyage, or early in their career. The huge *Great Republic*, for example, built by McKay in 1853 crossed from New York to the Scilly Islands in just thirteen days.

The *Sovereign of the Seas*, also built in 1853, made a crossing from New York to Liverpool in 13 days 23 hours with the best 24-hour run being 340 miles on that crossing. The *Donald McKay*, built in 1855, was another record breaker, making the passage from Boston to Cape Clear in Ireland in twelve days, but this run was particularly significant for a best 24-hour run of 421 miles. Many clipper ships were built for the British companies operating on the Australian clipper run: McKay's *Great Republic*, *Champion of the Seas*, *Lightning* and *James Baines* were all built for this route. The *Lightning*'s record for the best 24-hour run was 436 miles—which is an average speed of just over 18 knots, a remarkable performance for a sailing ship of over 100 years ago. The *James Baines* was one of the largest clipper ships to make the

Left Red Jacket *crossed from New York to Liverpool in just over thirteen days* (American Merchant Marine Museum).

Right Dreadnought *of the Black X Line—one of the most famous of the Atlantic packet ships* (American Merchant Marine Museum).

Atlantic crossing and set a record with a time of 12 days 6 hours from Boston to Liverpool. The same year, 1854, *Red Jacket* completed the New York-Liverpool run in a remarkable 13 days 1 hour.

One of the most famous of the big sailing ships regularly plying the Western Ocean was the *Dreadnought*. Built for the Red Cross Line of New York, this ship had an equally famous Captain, Samuel Samuels, one of the toughest skippers on the Atlantic, who became a legend in his own lifetime. He was so successful with earlier ships in the Red Cross Line that the *Dreadnought* was built specially for him and became known as the 'wild boat of the Atlantic'. Her first passage to Liverpool took 24 days but she made her reputation on the return voyage with a very fast passage of nineteen days. In December 1854 the *Dreadnought* crossed the Atlantic from New York to Liverpool in 13 days 11 hours, and five years later knocked another two hours off this time. Although these were not record crossings, the *Dreadnought*'s reputation came

from her consistently fast crossings in both directions. The all-time record for a packet or clipper ship crossing of the Atlantic was set in 1864 by the *Adelaide* with a time of 12 days 8 hours between New York and Liverpool.

The *Dreadnought* was the pride of the Red Cross Line but the company had far less success with their other ships and their toll of losses between 1850 and 1855 is indicative of the risks that were sometimes run. The *St Patrick* was wrecked in 1854 and the *Andrew Foster* was in collision in the Irish Sea and sank; the *Driver* was reported missing on the Atlantic with 600 people on board, whilst the *Racer* went ashore in the Irish Sea. It is a sorry record of disaster and perhaps this company had more than its fair share of bad luck. At this distance in time it is difficult to determine whether these losses were the result of the Captains taking extraordinary risks with their charges or whether other factors such as the unpredictable weather of the Atlantic Ocean come into play.

Despite these fast passages and the apparent regularity of the Atlantic services by the packet ships, the writing was on the wall. The threat posed by the steamships is shown significantly on the rare occasions when the sailing packet ships managed to make faster crossings than their rivals: in 1846 the packet boat *Toronto* arrived ahead of a Cunard steamer which had left the same day from England and the Captain became almost a national hero. The *Adelaide* of the Black Star Line in making her record passage across the Atlantic in 1864 beat the Cunard steamer *Sidonia* but this was

Above Glory of the Seas, *one of the fast clipper ships built by Donald McKay* (American Merchant Marine Museum).

Right *A view of the* Howard D Troop *in Atlantic waters. The reality apparent in such photographs of the sailing ships differs considerably from the romanticized paintings of the same vessels* (Sea Breezes).

a rare and notable achievement. Today's public may give its sympathy and affection to the sailing ship but the march of progress was inevitable. The speed and reliability of the steamships was steadily eclipsing the more erratic performance of the sailing packets and clipper ships. The sailing ships were fighting a losing battle for passengers and gradually they were switched to cargo carrying where they could still compete economically.

In the early days of the change over from sail the ocean-going steamships competed only on the transatlantic route and the fast sailing ships could still find passenger-carrying employment on the longer routes out to the Far East and Australia. As the size of sailing ships increased, wood construction gave way to iron and then steel thus losing the American shipyards building in wood the competitive edge that they had hitherto enjoyed against competing European yards. By 1880, however, the freight rates available for the sailing

The seven-masted schooner Thomas W. Lawson *which marked the swan song of the large sailing ship on the Atlantic at the turn of the century. She was finally wrecked off Land's End* (Sea Breezes).

ships had dropped drastically and sailing ships were increasingly relegated to the low class freights. Insurance rates for the softwood ships built in North America also rose, especially as they got older. Nevertheless the sailing ship took some time to die out on the Atlantic. The introduction of iron masts and rigging and later iron hulls allowed sailing ships to match the steamers in size. Even steam power was introduced on sailing ships, not to assist with propulsion (that would have turned them into steamships), but to help with the handling of the heavy sails and spars. Sail didn't die easily: iron and steel construction enabled much larger vessels to be built. The French five-masted barque *France*, for example, was built in 1918 with a length of 430 ft. In America, huge schooners were built: the *Thomas W. Lawson* built in steel in 1902 had no fewer than seven masts. The six-masted *Wyoming*, built in 1910, was the longest wooden sailing ship ever built with a length of 350 ft and represented a game attempt by the wooden shipyards to stay in the running but steam and steel had

really eclipsed their star by 1900.

Sailing ships continued to be seen on Atlantic waters up until the First World War and even in the 1920s and 1930s German and Scandinavian owners were still operating sailing vessels on the Atlantic, but they were a rarity, no more than a relic of the era when the Atlantic had been dominated by sail for both cargo and passenger trade. The best sailing ship in the world was no match for the speed and reliability of the steamer. The record passages made by the sailing ships of this era should be seen as a memorial to the thousands of passengers and crews who lost their lives in creating and maintaining the vital trade routes linking Old and New Worlds. The only sailing ships remaining today are training ships operated by a number of maritime nations and museum ships in permanent docks. The former maintain the illusion of the romance of sail, operating without commercial pressures, unrealistic relics of a bygone age. The latter give only a glimpse of the sailing ship life, the perils and uncertainties of its daily routine.

CHAPTER 4

Early steam

Steam has a long history as far as its use as a means of propulsion for boats and ships is concerned. The first developments took place in the 17th century. Towards the end of the 18th century steam-powered boats were being built in Europe and in America but these were for operating on rivers and canals and it was 1808 before the first steamship ventured out to sea. The *Phoenix* was designed for operating in the River Delaware but as she was built on the River Hudson she had to make a sea journey to get to her working territory. In Europe the *Comet* was launched in 1812 and operated first on the Clyde and then out to the Scottish islands.

Builders and operators of steamships became more adventurous and it was not long before they were looking at the possibility of crossing the Atlantic. The first steamship crossing was made in 1819 but here the word 'steamship' needs qualifying because the *Savannah* was designed as a sailing ship and only used her auxiliary engine for limited periods during the Atlantic crossing. Nevertheless the 320-ton *Savannah* has gone down in history as the first steamship to make the Atlantic crossing. Built

in New York in 1818 she was intended to operate the packet service from New York to Le Havre as a sailing ship but before she was completed she was purchased by the Savannah Steamship Company and fitted with a single-cylinder steam engine of 90 ihp. This engine drove the 15 ft diameter paddle wheels which were collapsible and could be stowed on deck when not in use. Speed under steam alone under fair conditions was a modest 4 knots.

With her steam engine and paddle wheels fitted the *Savannah* ran trials in March of 1819 but at that time her owners decided that the trade didn't justify her operation and it was decided to send her to Europe for sale. Loaded with 75 tons of coal, she set off on 24 May and after loading more coal at Kinsale in Ireland, she arrived in Liverpool on the 20 June having made an average speed of 6 knots. It is reported that the engines were in use for a total of only 85 hours during the passage. Although the *Savannah* made the crossing of the Atlantic from west to east, her claim to the title of the first steamship crossing must not be taken too literally, and although designed to carry passengers she didn't

The Savannah—*the first steamer to cross the Atlantic* (Mary Evans Picture Library).

actually have any on board during her Atlantic crossing!

The next ship fitted with steam power to cross the Atlantic was slightly bigger than the *Savannah* with a length of 123 ft. The *Rising Star* was built in London as a warship for use in the Chilean Revolution and was fitted with a twin-cylinder engine. The paddle wheels were incorporated inside the hull structure working through apertures in the bottom of the hull. She made the trip to Valparaiso, finally arriving in April 1822, after a voyage lasting nearly six months.

In 1824 the two-masted schooner *Caroline*, owned by the French navy, made a crossing of the Atlantic to French Guiana and later in 1827 made the return journey. This 121 ft vessel was fitted with a steam engine driving paddle wheels and she has the distinction of being the first steam vessel to make a two-way crossing of the Atlantic but once again the engine was used very much in the auxiliary mode, usually only brought into operation when the winds were ahead, under which conditions progress under power was painfully slow.

The first attempt to use a steamship as a trading vessel across the Atlantic came with the building of the *Calpe*. Built for American and Colonial Steam Navigation of London by a shipyard in Dover, this vessel was sold to the Dutch Navy in 1826 before she ever entered commercial service. However, she did make the passage across the Atlantic for her new owners in 1827 and went on to make two double crossings. Under Dutch ownership her name was changed to *Curacao*. Her paddle wheels were equipped with extensions which could be fitted at sea so that as the coal on board was burned up during a passage and the vessel rose in the water, the wheels would continue to dig into the water and push the vessel along. The next steam crossing of the Atlantic is also attributed to a naval vessel, this one being the paddle steamer *Rhadamanthus*, built for the

Royal Navy in 1832. Four sister ships were also built to a similar design at the same time but it was the *Rhadamanthus* which had the distinction of covering a distance of 2,500 miles across the Atlantic at a mean speed of 6.1 knots, but once again steam power was used only intermittently to help the vessel along during adverse winds or in calm conditions.

The *Royal William* became the first Canadian-built steamship to make the Atlantic crossing. The largest steamship at the time of her launch in 1831, she was designed to operate a regular passenger service between Quebec and Halifax. Samuel Cunard was one of the directors of the company. The *Royal William* operated successfully until she had to be quarantined following a cholera epidemic which caused a heavy financial loss for the company. Like the *Savannah* the *Royal William* was then sent to Europe for sale. On this crossing the ship carried seven passengers, the first to be carried across the Atlantic on a steamship, but the *Royal William*'s main claim to fame is the fact that she made virtually the whole crossing under steam power. Leaving Nova Scotia on 18 August 1833, *Royal William* encountered severe gales off Newfoundland which disabled the starboard engine and for ten days the port engine alone was used. She eventually arrived at her destination on the River Thames 25 days later after putting into the Isle of Wight for repairs. Her average speed on this crossing was 6 knots, despite having to stop for one day out of every four to clear the salt from the boilers. Like the majority of early steamships *Royal William* was not

fitted with condensers and therefore had to use salt water in the boilers.

In the short period of ten years these crossings of the Atlantic had demonstrated that the steamship services could be a viable proposition even on stormy northern waters. Steam engines were becoming more reliable, and no longer added to ships merely as an afterthought: ships like the *Royal William* were specifically designed from the keel up to accommodate steam engines and paddle wheels. The main problem was the provision of sufficient coal bunker space on board but on shorter routes steamships were soon operating regular and reliable passenger services and it was this experience which led to the almost simultaneous formation of three companies to operate transatlantic passenger services by steamship.

These companies, the British and American Steam Navigation Company of London, the Great Western Steamship Company of Bristol and the Transatlantic Steamship Company of Liverpool were the European answer to the American domination of transatlantic passenger traffic. British sailing ship companies had previously been concerned mainly with the emigrant trade, returning with non-human cargoes, leaving the prestigious packet ship routes to the Americans. The policies of these three companies reflect the rapid development of and confidence in steamships in Europe. All three companies were formed in 1838, a fact which generated intense competition to operate the first regular transatlantic steamship service. Each company had a steamship

The Sirius *was the first vessel to cross the Atlantic under continuous steam power. She is also the smallest steamer to cross the Atlantic having been built as an Irish Sea packet ship.* (Liverpool Maritime Museum).

designed and built for the transatlantic service, the *British Queen*, the *Great Western* and the *Liverpool* respectively. However, two companies decided not to wait for their new ships to be built and chartered ships to start the operation. This was an attempt to try and get a head start on the Great Western Steamship Company whose Brunel-designed *Great Western* had been launched in Bristol in 1837. The Transatlantic Steamship Company chartered the *Royal William* (not to be confused with the Canadian *Royal William*), and the British and American Steam Navigation Company chartered the *Sirius*, both these vessels having been built originally for the Irish cross-channel service.

The *Sirius* takes a place in history as being the first steamer to cross the Atlantic under continuous steam power, this 208 ft long vessel making the crossing from Cork to New York in 18 days 10 hours at a mean speed of 6.7 knots. Although she sailed from London, she called at Cork for refuelling and to pick up passengers. During this passage the *Great Western* was sighted on trials. The *Sirius* sailed from Cork on 3 April 1838 bound for New York. The *Great Western* sailed on the 8 April having been delayed for a day by unfavourable weather at Bristol. The *Great Western* arrived in New York on 23 April, only a few hours after the *Sirius*, but this margin of hours was enough to prevent the *Great Western* from receiving the accolade of being the first steamship to make the crossing of the Atlantic under steam alone.

Purpose-built to take on the North Atlantic, the *Great Western* was a magnificent ship for her day with a length of 236 ft. She made the Atlantic crossing in 15 days 5 hours with an average speed of 8 knots and gained consolation for the loss of her race with the *Sirius* at least with credit for having set a new speed record for the westbound crossing, beating by a comfortable margin any records set up before (or indeed after) this date by sailing ships. The *Great Western* set high standards of passenger accommodation which others sought to emulate. She had a magnificent main saloon, 75 ft long and 21 ft wide, and accommodation for eighty passengers in luxuriously appointed cabins. In comparison with strictly auxiliary power of the early Atlantic steamers, she had very powerful engines—with an indicated horsepower of 750. Coal consumption was 30 tons a day but the bunkers could hold up to 800 tons. The *Great Western* went on to complete 64 crossings of the North Atlantic and served her original builders until 1846 when she was sold to the Royal Mail Steam Packet Company Ltd, with whom she continued to operate Atlantic services between Southampton and the West Indies.

The *Royal William*, the other chartered ship to enter service on the Atlantic steamship routes and owned by the Transatlantic Steamship Company, made her departure from Liverpool, the first of a long line of passenger ships to adopt this port as its European terminal.

With 32 passengers on board she averaged 7.3 knots on her maiden voyage and completed three round trips on the Atlantic before returning once more to her Irish Sea service. The main distinction for which the *Royal William* is noted is that she is the smallest vessel ever to have steamed across the North Atlantic. With a length of 175 ft she was considerably smaller than the rival *Sirius*.

The second purpose-built Atlantic steamship to enter service was the *Liverpool*, built for and owned by the Transatlantic Steam Company. She left Liverpool on her maiden voyage in the autumn of 1838 with sixty passengers on board intent on a non-stop crossing, but was forced into Cork by a violent gale. It was sixteen days from her Liverpool departure before she finally left Ireland, covering the journey to New York at an average speed of 7.9 knots. The *Liverpool* was the first two-funnelled steamer to take on the Atlantic but her operations were not a success and the Transatlantic Steamship Company was wound up two years after formation.

The *British Queen* was purpose-built for the British and American Steam Navigation Company and at the time of her launch in 1838 was the largest steamship afloat. Accommodation was provided for 207 passengers with 104 berths in the aft cabins and 103 in forward cabins. A large 60 ft long dining saloon was situated between the two cabin areas. Completion of this vessel was delayed by the financial problems of the engine builders and the *British Queen* did not finally sail from London until 1839, making her departure for New York

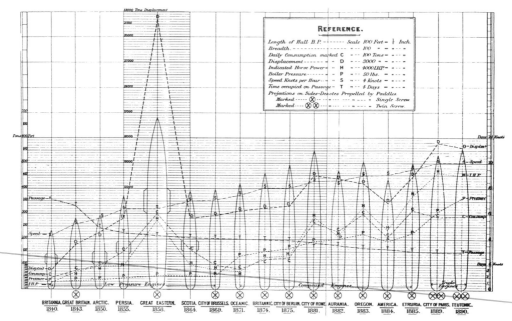

The growth of the Atlantic liner between 1840 and 1890.

from Portsmouth. She averaged 8.4 knots on her maiden voyage across the Atlantic, and made nine crossings in the service of the British and American Steam Navigation Company before being sold to the Belgian government under whose auspices she continued in Atlantic service until 1842.

It is interesting to note that even at this early stage in development the size of the steamships had quite rapidly overtaken the average size of sailing ships operating on the Atlantic routes. One reason for this was the need to accommodate a large quantity of coal in bunkers to sustain the boilers on the long Atlantic crossing. Early steamships were actually limited to passenger carrying or military uses because once the bunkers

had been loaded there was very little space available for cargo. By contrast passengers were (relative to cargo) light in weight and their accommodation could be built over and around the space required for engines, boilers and bunkers.

Although steam power was used continuously on these crossings, all early steamships were fitted with a full inventory of masts and sails and obviously used these to the fullest extent when winds were favourable. These early ships were all paddle steamers built in wood and must have experienced considerable difficulty keeping the paddle wheels in the water when the ship was rolling in any sort of seaway. Contemporary reports suggest that there was continual trouble with paddle wheels being damaged and repairs having to be effected at sea. On the other hand the problem of salt contamination in the boilers had largely been removed by the introduction of condensers which allowed fresh water to be recirculated throughout the system. Nevertheless machinery on these early ships was not particularly efficient with steam pressures for example rarely exceeding 5 lb per square inch. The engines themselves were massive, with the bore and stroke being measured in feet rather than inches, and it is a remarkable testimony to the early engineering skills that the machinery could cope with the stresses and strains of an Atlantic crossing. In addition to the risk from the ravages of Atlantic weather, there was also a considerable fire risk on these wooden-hulled vessels.

The pioneer steamships on the Atlantic service captured the imagination of the public in a way which was to continue for more than a century through all the magnificent Atlantic liners which were to follow. The departure of ships on their maiden voyages attracted huge crowds and their arrival in New York set the precedent for the receptions afforded later to all major new passenger ships making their first appearance in the harbour. The rivalry of the *Sirius* and the *Great Western* and their arrival within hours of each other in New York continued a trend set by the sailing packet ships and firmly established the pattern of Atlantic 'races' which intensified the competition between operating companies.

On one occasion in 1839 the *British Queen* and the *Great Western* sailed from New York on the same day, but this time it was Brunel's ship which arrived home first in Bristol, but only hours ahead of the *British Queen*'s arrival in Portsmouth. In time such rivalry between ships and companies developed into a matter of national pride involving governments and politicians in the struggle for supremacy on the oceans. Fast passages and luxurious accommodation were the criteria by which Atlantic passenger ships were judged: safety, caution and respect for the ocean appear to have taken a back seat.

One of the greatest names in passenger shipping was that of Samuel Cunard whose direct association with the Atlantic really began when he won the contract for the carriage of mail by steamship across the North Atlantic in 1838 (although he had also been linked with the *Royal William*). At that time he didn't have a ship with which to fulfil his obligations, but with this contract in his pocket Cunard formed the British and North American Royal Mail Steam Packet Company, later to become the Cunard Steamship Company, and the paddle steamer *Unicorn* (which had been built in 1836) was purchased to operate the embryonic mail service. The *Unicorn*'s first Atlantic crossing took place in 1840 with 27 passengers on board, and the ship reached Halifax in fourteen days, averaging 8 knots in what are described as appalling weather conditions.

The 185 ft-long *Unicorn* was kept on to operate a service between Quebec,

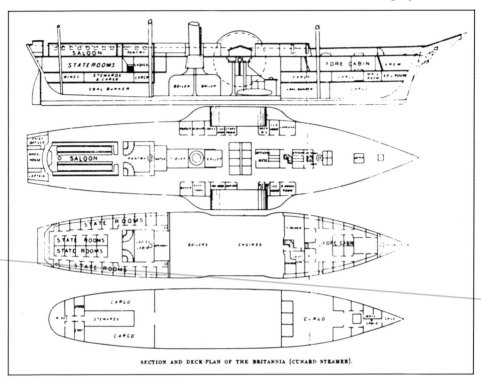

SECTION AND DECK-PLAN OF THE BRITANNIA (CUNARD STEAMER).

Plans of the Cunard steamer Britannia *built in 1840.*

Pictou and Halifax while the Cunard Line had four new ships, the *Britannia, Acadia, Caledonia* and *Columbia*, built to maintain the Atlantic service. With four ships in his Atlantic fleet, Cunard brought a new pattern to the Atlantic passenger trade: the four vessels established a monthly transatlantic mail steamship service between Liverpool, Halifax and Boston. The first of these vessels to enter service was the *Britannia* but the other ships were of almost identical design. With a length of 207 ft these ships didn't break any size records but when built in 1840 they offered a new

degree of sophistication, particularly in the machinery. The steam pressure was now raised to 9 lb per square inch to supply the 440 hp engines. Although the speed of the vessel is given as 8.5 knots the *Britannia* made her maiden voyage from Liverpool to Halifax in 11 days 4 hours to give a mean speed of 10 knots—perhaps indicating that she must have had considerable help from the wind on this crossing. The *Britannia* was received with great enthusiasm in both Halifax and Boston, these ports being delighted to be on the receiving end of a passenger service which was eclipsing the service provided by the sailing packet ships departing from New York. On the return voyage to Liverpool the *Britannia* took just over ten days for the crossing, a record for any vessel at that time.

Much was made of the regularity and reliability of these passenger services, but aboard such comparatively small ships the North Atlantic must still have been quite uncomfortable at times, particularly during winter storms. The hazards of nature which had plagued sailing ships such as ice and fog, particularly over the Grand Banks and the waters down to Nova Scotia, did not suddenly disappear, so perhaps it was almost inevitable that eventually disaster would strike.

In 1843 the *Columbia* ran aground on rocks off Cape Sable at the south-east tip of Nova Scotia, but, amazingly, all the passengers and crew were saved *as well as* the mail and cargo! Even before this incident Cunard had ordered a further ship of a larger size, the *Hibernia*, and after the loss of the *Columbia* he ordered a sixth ship, the *Cambria*. These two new ships were faster and more luxurious than the first four and for seven years the Cunard Line had a virtual monopoly of transatlantic steamship service. Even so services were not profitable and it was only the mail subsidies which enabled operations to continue. Despite this lack of profit it was inevitable that Cunard supremacy would eventually be challenged and that the challenge would come from the United States.

It was the proposed award of mail contracts from the United States

---

The Collins Line ship Arctic *held the Blue Riband for four years from 1851, but sank after a collision off Newfoundland* (Sea Breezes).

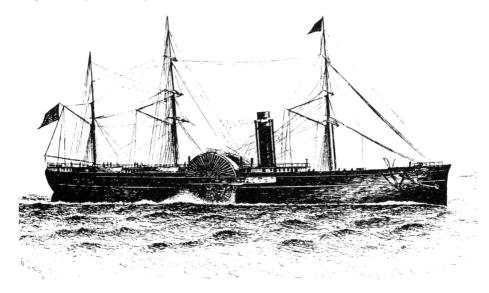

The Baltic, *one of four sister ships built for the Collins Line in 1850. She set a new westbound record in 1851 with a speed of 13.17 knots* (American Merchant Marine Museum).

Government which prompted the construction of the paddle steamer *Washington* by the US company Ocean Steam Navigation Company in 1847. When she was commissioned the *Washington* became the largest ship afloat and was reputed to be the fastest. On her first sailing from New York, with 120 passengers on board, she found herself racing the Cunard liner *Britannia* which left Boston on the same day for Liverpool. The *Britannia* completed the crossing two days ahead of her rival but since New York to Southampton is a considerably longer distance than Boston to Liverpool there can have been little difference in the speed of the two vessels. In fact the *Washington's* performance was quite creditable considering that this was her maiden voyage. A second ship, the

Hermann, was added to the Ocean Steam Navigation Company fleet in 1848 and made a record crossing from New York to Southampton in 11 days 21 hours.

Not to be outdone by this American competition, Cunard obtained a contract to operate a Liverpool to New York route and alternated this on a weekly basis with Halifax and Boston. Four new ships were built to maintain this service, the *America, Niagara, Europa* and *Canada*. The last two ships set new Atlantic records on their Liverpool to New York crossings with the *Canada* taking just 9 days 22 hours to cross from Liverpool to Boston. Cunard supremacy was re-established but the Americans were not taking things lying down and with support from naval sources the Collins Line was established to build five large and fast mail steamers for the Atlantic routes. The *Atlantic* was the first of these to be built (in 1849) with a length of 300 ft, but construction was still in wood. She was followed by the *Pacific, Arctic*, and *Baltic*, while a fifth ship was planned but never built. Luxurious accommodation for 200 passengers was provided but these vessels could also carry 450 tons of cargo and were powered by engines of 800 hp. The *Atlantic* left on her maiden crossing in 1850 but suffered considerable problems, only managing to redeem herself on the return voyage with a record run of 10 days 16 hours to beat the Cunard record. Cunard retaliated with even faster speeds from their ships and as the pace increased so further casualties occurred. The SS *Atlantic* was an early victim. She was overdue on a mid-winter voyage until she was sighted by a Cunard ship, her main paddle shaft broken. With only sail power available the ship had to return to Cork. Attempts to set new records did not diminish and the four Collins Line ships dominated the Atlantic with crossings in less than ten days to gain what became known as the Blue Riband—a title given in later years to all speed record holders and believed to have its origin in the blue of the garter sash worn by Knights of the Garter. Average speeds for a crossing soon rose to around 13 knots and

The Cunard paddle steamer Arabia, *the last wooden vessel built for Cunard, was launched in 1851* (American Merchant Marine Museum).

the effect of speed on passenger traffic can be seen by the fact that patronage of the slower Cunard ships fell by 50 per cent while Collins held the record.

Cunard tried to tackle this problem by commissioning the *Arabia* but this wooden paddle steamer could not compete with the all-conquering Collins Line ships. The stage seemed set for Collins' dominance when the Cunard ships were taken out of Atlantic service after requisition by the British Admiralty for military use during the Crimea War. In 1854, then, the Collins Line ships had the trans-ocean routes to themselves when disaster struck and the *Arctic* collided with the 200-ton steamer *Vesta* in dense fog sixty miles south of Newfoundland. The *Vesta* made port safely. It was only after she had steamed away that the *Arctic* realized that damage was so extensive tht the ship was sinking fast. The Captain headed for Cape Race in an attempt to beach the ship, but it sank twenty miles from land. Only a handful

of the 391 passengers and crew survived in the two lifeboats: there was public condemnation of the high speeds of record-breaking ships in fog, but little comment was made about the lack of lifeboats. Two years later in 1856 the *Pacific* was also lost at sea and despite the fitting of additional watertight bulkheads on the *Baltic*, the Collins Line could not cope with the adverse publicity of these disasters and collapsed in 1858.

The way was open for Cunard to make a comeback and this they did with a vengeance by introducing the *Persia* in 1855. The first iron vessel for the company and the first iron paddle steamer on the Atlantic routes, she also represented a big leap forward in size being 376 ft in length. More attention was paid to safety features in an attempt to restore public confidence in Atlantic liners. The *Persia* crossed the Atlantic from Liverpool to New York at a speed of 13.82 knots, giving her the Blue Riband which she held until 1862.

New companies operating steamships entered the North Atlantic passenger trade. Notable newcomers included the Inman Line from Britain, and the Hamburg Amerika Line from Germany. With the Collins Line in decline, American hopes shifted to the Vanderbilt European Line established by Cornelius Vanderbilt. This service was originally begun with the *North Star* which was Vanderbilt's own 2,000-ton private yacht, but the reputation of the company was established by the purpose-built *Vanderbilt* launched in 1855 which came close to setting a new Atlantic record but could not quite break the supremacy of the Cunarders.

The switch by Cunard to iron as a construction material for their trans-Atlantic liners was overshadowed by the introduction of screw propulsion in 1843. The SS *Great Britain* was the first screw-propelled vessel and the first vessel built of iron to cross the Atlantic. Built in Bristol for the Great Western Steam-

ship Company she was notable for her technological innovation and her length of 322 ft, but was overshadowed on the Atlantic routes by the faster paddle steamers. The SS *Great Britain* left Liverpool for her maiden crossing in 1845 but her Atlantic days ended abruptly when she was stranded on the coast of Ireland. After being aground for eleven months she was refloated and moved to the Australian service. Nevertheless, the design of the *Great Britain* set the pattern for future successful Atlantic liners. By contrast her sister the *Great Eastern*, built in 1858, has been described as the most ambitious failure in the whole history of naval architecture. Five times the tonnage of any ship then in use she was close to 700 ft in length. A hybrid screw and paddle wheel system of propulsion was proposed for this monster to give her a speed of 15 knots. The advantage of size was that sufficient bunkers could be carried for very long passages and there was accommodation too for 4,000 passen-

gers. The *Great Eastern* left Southampton in 1860 on her maiden voyage to New York, but her speed did not come up to expectations. The vessel was never a commercial success as a passenger vessel and between 1865 and 1873 she was used to lay a number of transatlantic cables. The size of the *Great Eastern* was not to be exceeded for another forty years. The last wooden steamship built for Atlantic passenger service was the *Adriatic* built for the Collins Line in 1856. Five years later saw the last of the paddle steamers, the *Scotia*, enter Atlantic service.

The American Civil War greatly curtailed Atlantic passenger traffic and it was not until 1863 that the *Scotia* set a new Atlantic record with a crossing from New York to Cork at an average speed of 14 knots. On the westward crossing she set a speed of 14.54 knots and both records lasted until 1867. The Cunard Line stuck to paddle steamers because their contract with the Admiralty for carrying mail had stipulated the use of paddle steamers. Eventually the Admiralty relented and Cunard were able to introduce their first screw steamer, the *Russia*, which set a new record on the eastbound crossing with a speed of 14.22 knots.

The Inman Line saw a market niche in the emigrant trade to America, leaving to Cunard the first class passengers. The Inman Line's *City of Glasgow* has been described as the prototype of the modern ocean steamship and the *City of Paris*, built in 1865, took the Blue Riband in 1867. When the *Russia* and the *City of Paris* left New York together they made their crossings of the Atlantic within minutes of each other. The Inman Line was riding high by 1870 but then came the White Star Line which commissioned four ships to be built for the Atlantic trade, the *Oceanic, Atlantic, Baltic* and *Republic*. The *Baltic* set a new Atlantic record in 1873, and made history by being the first ship to exceed an average speed of 15 knots on the Atlantic crossing. Success, however, was marred by the loss of the SS *Atlantic* three months later. Five days out from Liverpool the *Atlantic* ran into wild gales which caused her to reduce speed. With bunkers dwindling and still 460 miles to go, the Captain decided to put into Halifax for more coal. Reputedly without adequate charts and little experience of the port approaches, the *Atlantic* went aground some twenty miles from Halifax and over half of the nearly 1,000 passengers and crew on board lost their lives. A letter written in 1875 and

Top left *The* Scotia *was the last and the finest paddle steamer built for the Cunard line. Launched in 1861 she held the Blue Riband from 1862 to 1867* (Liverpool Maritime Museum).

Above left *The second* City of Paris, *built for the Inman Line in 1889. This twin-screw liner of 10,479 tons captured the Blue Riband in both directions in 1889* (Liverpool Maritime Museum).

Left *The* Paris, *formerly the* City of Paris, *aground on the Manacles Rocks off Cornwall in 1899. This Blue Riband holder was refloated and gave more than twenty years further service before finally being scrapped in 1923.*

with an innovative propeller shaft, incorporating a universal joint which allowed the propeller to be lowered deeper into the water to prevent it racing in heavy seas but after several voyages this system was replaced by a more conventional installation. In 1876 the *Germanic* set a new Atlantic speed record which was later broken by her sister, after *Britannic*'s propeller had been changed. These two ships now captured public interest and again put the White Star Line in the forefront of ocean travel.

The Guion Line had been operating on the Atlantic for thirteen years before they decided in 1876 to build a ship to attempt the Blue Riband. The result was the *Arizona* which upped the record speed to 15.96 knots, a record which she held for three years. In an accident which highlighted the risks involved in the Atlantic crossing, she collided with an iceberg in 1879 whilst travelling at 14 knots, and although her bow was crushed for a length of 26 ft, a collision bulkhead saved her from sinking. After putting into St Johns, Newfoundland, a temporary wooden bow was fitted and the liner continued her voyage to Liverpool.

In 1881 the Cunard Line made a brief reappearance in the record charts with the first steel ship on the Atlantic routes, the *Servia*. The Guion Line responded with the largest ship then in service, the *Oregon*. This vessel was still shorter by a considerable margin than the *Great Eastern*, but she set a new Atlantic record taking the average speed up to 17.48 knots. Despite this success the Guion Line were running into financial

difficulty and the *Oregon* was sold to arch-rivals Cunard, for whom she went on to set further records.

From 1880 or so to the end of the century a ding-dong battle started for the Atlantic speed record with the prestigious title of 'fastest on the Atlantic' changing hands almost every year. The *America* built for the National Line of Liverpool took the title from the *Oregon* but then lost it back to the (now) Cunard ship. The *Oregon* was involved in a collision off Fire Island, New York, in 1886 from which she eventually sank but the passengers and crew were rescued by the Norddeutscher liner *Fulda*. This was Cunard's first major ship casualty on the North Atlantic for many years, but rescue of everyone aboard preserved the reputation of the company in the public's eye. Cunard maintained their service with the *Etruia* and the *Umbria*, the former ship coming very close to breaking the 20-knot barrier with a speed of 19.9 knots for an eastbound crossing in 1887. It was the second *City of Paris*, however, owned by the Inman Line which finally crossed this threshold in 1889 on a westbound crossing, going on to break the 20-knot barrier on the eastbound crossing as well later the same year. Two years later the new White Star Line twins *Teutonic* and *Majestic* each held the westbound Atlantic record for brief periods. These two famous sister ships claim a special place among the distinguished ranks of the Atlantic liners. They were the first White Star liners to have twin screws but they were also the last ships to be ordered by this company to attempt the Blue Riband.

By the turn of the century the whole concept of Atlantic liners was changing: lengths steadily increased and much more reliance was placed on the engines, with sails being very much an auxiliary feature or even abandoned entirely. Many vessels now had at least twin screws and it was increasingly felt that engines were sufficiently reliable on their own to the point that sails could be discarded. With speeds approaching 20 knots, the windage of the masts and rigging also detracted from the speed potential.

To the public, however, the main development with this new breed of liner was the appointment of ever more luxurious accommodation. The *Teutonic* and her sister ship, *Majestic*, were especially impressive in this respect. These ships were seen as epitomizing national pride for although the Guion Line's *City of New York* and *City of Paris* raced under the British flag, the company and their ships were to all intents and purposes American owned. The rivalry between these four ships aroused tremendous public interest. Cunard tried to stand publicly aloof but they were equally guilty of forcing their ships to maintain schedules no matter what conditions the Atlantic threw up. On one occasion the *City of New York* and the *Teutonic* left Cork almost simultaneously and arrived at New York within four hours of each other, the *Teutonic* setting the pace and claiming a new Atlantic record.

The Inman Line eventually transferred to the United States flag in 1893 in order to qualify for a subsidy to carry American mails. The new American company was called the International Navigation Company, later to become known as the American Line from which stable a Blue Riband holder was to emerge in the following century. Cunard, meantime, commissioned two new ships for the Atlantic route, the *Lucania* and the *Campania*. Completed in 1893 both went straight out to set new records on the Atlantic, taking the record close to 22 knots. Up until this time all the Atlantic records had been held by either British or American ships, but in the next year or two began the challenge from German ships.

The importance of the Atlantic record to national pride is demonstrated by the German move into the arena in 1897. For over forty years all of the Blue Riband holders had been constructed in British yards and even the early ships of Norddeutscher Lloyd and the Hamburg Amerika Line were built in Britain, but when it came to building Blue Riband contenders, national pride dictated that ships be built in home yards. By 1897 the two German companies were carrying considerably more passengers across the Atlantic than the British. This was largely due to the huge numbers of German emigrants seeking new lives in America who formed a captive market for the German vessels. But the German companies were also determined to compete for the cream of the passenger trade—which meant building large and fast liners. Two ships were built for this challenge: the *Kaiser Wilhelm der Grosse* and the slightly smaller *Kaiser Friedrich*. The *Kaiser Wilhelm der Grosse* with a length of 627 ft was the largest passenger

liner in the world at the time of her launch, and, as events were to prove, also the fastest. Her machinery comprised two sets of four-cylinder triple-expansion steam engines producing a total of 28,000 ihp. To supply these engines coal consumption was a massive 250 tons a day and the design speed of the ship was 22.5 knots. On her maiden voyage, the liner didn't quite match up to these speeds or the record speeds which had been set by Cunard's pair *Campania* and *Lucania*, but towards the end of 1897 she managed an eastbound crossing at an average speed of 22.35 knots and a year later set a westbound record of just over 23 knots.

As further competition entered the arena the shipping companies found themselves treading an even narrower line between operating advertised services on schedule and avoiding the bad publicity which would result from any accident. In the latter part of the 19th century the mixture of sailing ships and fast steam ships on the Atlantic was an unhealthy one. Some of the sailing ships which disappeared without trace at this time could have been victims of collision with steamships—which would, perhaps, hardly have noticed the impact as they thundered across the Atlantic. Sailing ships were generally reluctant to carry lights and invariably the steamships would come off best in such encounters, a fact symbolic, perhaps, of the fact that by the outbreak of the First World War steamships had most certainly replaced sailing vessels as the prime movers of people and cargoes across the Atlantic Ocean.

The heyday of the liners

The twenty years between 1890 and 1910 saw the Atlantic Liner come of age. With the liners now approaching 700 ft in length passengers were, at last, largely isolated from the rigours of going to sea, or so at least the liner companies would have their customers believe. They did everything in their power to surround passengers with all the comforts of the shore so that the risks would appear minimal and they could pretend that the often violent weather of the North Atlantic Ocean could be shrugged off with impunity.

The reality was otherwise of course, because no matter what size the ship, the storms outside could not be shrugged off or ignored and as average speeds rose above 20 knots the ability to maintain speed and schedules in rough seas became more difficult. This was particularly true on westbound crossings when ships were ploughing into prevailing westerlies. The fine bows of even the largest liners would be totally submerged in the oncoming seas and tons of water would roar down the deck to crash dangerously against the superstructure. Damage to the fittings and fixtures on the decks was a common occurrence and

ought to have served as a warning to Captains that the time had come to slow down. It was a message that continued to be ignored by some masters in the interests of making a fast passage. Serious damage to the bridge structure through wave impact was a disturbing feature of some of the more dramatic crossings. This type of damage, however, rarely put the ships' very survival at risk; but balancing the demands of the shipowners for regular schedules to be maintained and the dictates of safety, which demanded that ships eased down when the sea was rough, remained a problem for masters and senior crew members. There is little warning, as any seaman will know, when you have gone over the edge, and the bow descends into the first large wave: 40 and 50 ft waves are not uncommon in Atlantic storms, and the mightiest ship could soon be dwarfed.

In severe weather, more responsible crews would try to keep the motion of the vessel to a minimum to ensure passenger comfort—an extremely difficult task when plunging into a heavy head sea, trying to maintain speed and schedule and avoid damage to the ship's superstructure. The elite accommodation was placed amidships where the motion was generally least but passengers would always be aware of violent pitching into a head sea. If the sea was on the beam then a rolling effect would be experienced and before the days of computer-controlled stabilizers Captains could only alter course to reduce the movement. Passenger loyalty with the liner companies was only as good as the last trip across and a passenger who had suffered discomfort on one trip would think nothing of switching his or her allegiance to another line in the hope of better treatment. Few who were not professional seamen would appreciate that all vessels were and are the same to the might of an Atlantic storm.

Higher speeds tended to negate the improvements in passenger comfort that were made possible by increases in vessel size. Captains would always have to balance speed, comfort and safety, and their problems were often exacerbated by the design of the liners in their charge. The demand for high speed meant that the hull had to have fine lines, and fine lines do not make for particularly seaworthy ships: a fine bow lacks the buoyancy to rise to an oncoming wave and was much more likely to go through it than over it. Fine lines also make a ship less stable and more prone to rolling. Yet speed remained the overwhelming prime requirement in design, and compromises made by the naval architects would always be biased in this direction.

Navigation, never the easiest of arts of the Atlantic, remained a problem as speeds rose. By the beginning of the 20th

century the sextant and the chronometer had been fully refined, so that observations could give positions with a good degree of accuracy, certainly to within one mile given reasonable conditions. But the North Atlantic doesn't always know the meaning of the phrase and skies are more often overcast than not, and overcast skies do not allow sights to be taken. As crossing times tumbled down to five days or so a liner might get no more than one or two fixes on the way across the Atlantic and yet she would be expected to make an accurate landfall on schedule. On the European side landfalls were made slightly easier even in modest visibility, because the majority of dangerous rocks were marked by lighthouses by this time, but on the American side, the Nantucket Shoals stretching fifty miles out to sea from Nantucket Island were one of many traps waiting to close on unwary vessels as they neared the land on the way into New York. Even in fine weather an accurate landfall here is difficult, but in fog it must have been a nightmare. Approaching land on either side of the Atlantic in poor visibility in a large liner at speeds around 20 knots, with thousands of passengers on board and working on dead reckoning from positions two or three days old, must have taxed the navigation skills of any ship's officers to the maximum.

Radar which could help to fix positions in fog was non-existent until after the Second World War. A large ship travelling at 20 knots takes several miles to be brought to a stop and even if ships slowed down as they were supposed to in fog, then their very size

The Titanic *heads down the River Clyde to begin trials before the start of her disastrous maiden voyage* (US Coast Guard).

and momentum could still make it difficult to take avoiding action should other vessels suddenly loom out of the fog. It is therefore hardly surprising that there were numerous collisions between the liners and other ships. The White Star liner *Olympic* collided with HMS *Hawke* when approaching Southampton on 20 September 1907, but escaped with comparatively minor damage. Perhaps because the liner invariably came off best in these encounters, with relatively superficial damage, they received little publicity and little adverse comment was made.

Several liners struck icebergs in their haste. The highly publicized sinking of the *Titanic* in 1912, could almost have been predicted long before the event occurred, for several earlier ships suffered collision and damage. In 1907 the *Kronprinz Wilhelm* was travelling at 16 knots when she struck an iceberg a glancing blow—and was lucky to do so, for at that speed a more direct impact could have resulted in very severe damage. In 1911, less than one year before the *Titanic* went down, the Anchor Line ship *Colombia* hit an iceberg on her way from Glasgow to New York. The Captain's terse message over the radio was: 'August 4th 1911—180 miles east Cape Race. During intermittent fog collided with iceberg, damage bow, proceeding on voyage, weather fine, position today noon—43 degrees 40 north—28 degrees 22 west. Signed Mitchell.'

The *Colombia* was fortunate because she had slowed to 8 knots in the known iceberg region. Even so, when she hit the berg the bow plunged 12 ft into the ice and tons of ice fell on to the deck. The liner was carrying 520 passengers and although none suffered injury, this must

One of the 'Incomparables', the Mauretania *on trials* (Swan Hunter Shipbuilding).

The result was the commissioning of two of the most famous ships ever to sail the Atlantic, the *Lusitania* and *Mauretania*. These ships were the largest and fastest on the Atlantic route to date with a length of 790 ft and a design speed of 24.5 knots. By any stretch of the imagination these were superships and when the *Mauretania* reached 27.4 knots on trials and then set a new Atlantic record, soon after her launch, it came as no surprise. What is amazing is that she was to hold this record for an unprecedented 22 years. Both vessels made use of steam turbines for the propulsion machinery. Up to this time virtually all liners had been built with compound reciprocating steam engines but with a massive 70,000 hp being required to propel the *Lusitania* and *Mauritania* at their design speeds, steam turbines seemed the logical answer. The most powerful turbines previously fitted to ships were the 12,000 hp engines of the liners *Victoria* and *Virginian* of the Allan Line built in 1904. To make the quantum step up to the huge power output required for the new ships was a very brave step indeed, but one that was amply rewarded.

The *Lusitania* was the first of the twins to take to the water and almost immediately set a new Atlantic record, but she was outclassed by her sister's maiden voyge. The *Mauretania* set several records on the Atlantic and was the first surface vessel to complete a crossing in under five days. One round trip from Liverpool to New York and back again was completed in under twelve days and the *Mauretania* was the vehicle aboard which *Daily Mail* correspondent, W.R. Holt, made a 7,000 mile journey at an average speed of 23 mph for the whole twelve-day trip. On this occasion the *Mauretania* even made a special call at Fishguard to land Mr. Holt who was then conveyed to London by a special train.

Once more the Cunard Line was back in control on the Atlantic and in recognition of this, when the White Star Line ordered two new ships for the Atlantic service the *Olympic* and the *Titanic*, they opted for size rather than speed. These two ships had a length of 882 ft, nearly 100 ft longer than the *Mauretania*, but the trial speed was only 21.75 knots and no attempt at Atlantic speed records was ever made with these liners. Sadly the *Titanic* only achieved fame and even notoriety through her highly publicized collision with an iceberg in 1912 when over 1,500 lives were lost. This appalling disaster was to have a lasting affect on all forms of shipping with new legislation regarding lifeboats and safety equipment on ships and the establishment of the International Ice Patrol being positive actions to accrue from a maritime disaster of unprecedented proportion. But even after 1912 and despite the obvious risks from icebergs, there was little attempt to force the Atlantic liners clear of ice areas and steamship routes continued to be dictated by the shipping companies and ship masters rather than by legislation.

Many vessels making record attempts would deviate from the officially recommended routes in order to make faster passages, but there was little reason for the *Titanic* to make such a change of course, because with her limited speed potential there was no possibility of her making a record crossing. What is surprising with the *Titanic* disaster is the fact that she did not significantly slow her speed, despite

The fine bows of the Mauretania *were designed to slice through the Atlantic waves* (Swan Hunter Shipbuilding).

The damaged bridge of the Lusitania *after being struck by a freak wave in 1910—tarpaulins cover the smashed windows and steelwork. The second view shows the interior of the bridge with timbers shoring up the structure* (Frank O. Braynard collection).

warnings about ice in her vicinity. The Cunard liner *Carmania* run into an area of icebergs interspersed with growlers and smaller ice and was brought to a halt. The French liner *Niagara* had also run into this ice field, apparently some 70 by 35 miles in area, and had been damaged both below and above the waterline. Her crew managed to stem these leaks with temporary patching and the ship and her 100 passengers completed the voyage. Certainly this icefield was a major hazard to shipping in the North Atlantic and in addition to the three liners which ran into trouble, there are reports of numerous other ships either being entrapped in this ice or in collision with icebergs.

Meanwhile, the *Lusitania* and her sister in the Cunard fleet, *Mauretania*, were not without problems. *Mauretania* demonstrated a tendency to plough into head seas, often pitching quite violently. On one occasion the *Lusitania* shipped an enormous sea over the bow which broke in the wheelhouse windows and bent the steel of the superstructure. Several of the lifeboats were smashed in this incident—and the wheelhouse on the *Lusitania* was 80 ft above the waterline. Both ships also rolled much more heavily than anticipated, despite company blandishments that all was sweetness and light on these wonderful new liners. Despite their problems, which also included the loss of one of the *Mauretania*'s propeller blades in 1908, these two magnificent liners became known as 'The Incomparables'. They dominated the Atlantic service until the First World War during which (in 1915) the *Lusitania* was torpedoed and sunk by a German U-boat with the loss of 1,198 lives. In 1913 the pair had been joined by the *Aquitania*,

Above *The* Aquitania *at speed.*

Below *The counter stern of the* Aquitania.

which was the first liner to exceed 900 ft
in length. Despite her impressive length,
the *Aquitania* never matched the speed
and performance of 'The Incomparables' and her fastest crossing at 25 knots
was well below the record set by the
Mauretania.

In 1914 on the outbreak of war, an
even larger liner was being built in Germany to bring that nation back into the
reckoning for the Blue Riband. Built
and launched as the *Bismarck* in 1914,
this ship was not finally completed until
1922 when it was handed over to the
White Star Line as part of a war reparations deal and renamed *Majestic.* She was
the largest ship on the Atlantic for many
years (at 954 ft in length), but she never
managed to break any records, despite
a design speed above 25 knots. The
White Star Line tended to be more concerned with size than speed, and back in
1911 they had proposed the construction
of a new ship, the *Gigantic,* which was to
have a length in excess of 1,000 ft and a
beam of 112 ft, designed to carry over

4,000 passengers. With twelve decks, the proposed design included facilities for golf, tennis and cricket matches, but this boat was to be no ocean greyhound and was planned to make leisurely seven-day crossings of the Atlantic. In reporting the possibility of building this ship, *The New York Times* noted: 'There are no technical difficulties about building a ship with these unprecedented dimensions, but there are commercial difficulties and new docks would have to be built to take ships of this size.' Presumably these economic factors and the gathering clouds of war prevented the ship from ever being built.

The war set back German attempts to increase their shre of the lucrative Atlantic passenger trade, but the nation defeated on the battlefield was not to be outdone in her quest for the Atlantic Blue Riband. In 1928 the *Bremen* and the *Europa* were launched with the specific objective of wresting the title from the *Mauretania*. This was achieved in a convincing manner in 1929 when the 938 ft

Bremen made her maiden voyage across the Atlantic at an average speed of 27.83 knots. With 130,000 hp available to her, the *Bremen* and her slightly larger sister *Europa* dominated the Atlantic passenger routes, and in 1934 raised the record to 28 knots. These two ships set new standards of passenger accommodation and provided all sorts of new facilities although many of them had been anticipated in the design of the *Gigantic*. Swimming pools, a sports arena, ballroom, cinema and shopping centres were all available to passengers. When the *Europa* joined the *Bremen* in 1930 she captured the Blue Riband with a speed of 27.91 knots on the westward crossing, but in 1933 the record went back to the *Bremen* when she raised the speed to 28.51 knots.

German domination could not go unchallenged, and as both France and Italy determined to enter the competition, a fresh adversary was developing in Britain. Indeed, the early 1930s saw intense activity in the offices of naval architects around Europe and the stage was being set for the most competitive period ever in the history of the Atlantic liner. Cunard Line had been resting on the laurels of the *Mauretania* and the *Aquitania* for many years but in December 1930 work began on vessel no 534, later to be named *Queen Mary*, at John Brown's shipyard on Clydeside. A few weeks later the keel of the French liner *Normandie* was laid, and earlier that year work had started in Italy on two superliners, the *Rex* and the *Conte di Savoia*. Although ordered together, the two Italian ships were quite different in character: though the *Conte di Savoia* was a fine vessel the larger and faster *Rex* was clearly designed to take the Blue Riband. The Atlantic crossing for an Italian ship began at Gibraltar and ended at New York. In 1933 the *Rex*, which operated out of Genoa, completed this passage in four and a half days—at an average speed of 28.92 knots. Trials with this ship had come close to the magic 30 knot mark, but she never managed to sustain this sort of speed on Atlantic crossings.

Both the Italian and the French liner building programmes continued during the economic recession of the early 1930s, despite the severe effect that this had on Atlantic passenger traffic. In Britain the Great Depression led to the postponement of the building of the *Queen Mary* and construction was halted for 27 months. It had been the Cunard

tradition to build Atlantic liners in pairs, but government funding for two vessels was only forthcoming after the enforced merger of the Cunard and the White Star companies. That second vessel was later to become famous as the *Queen Elizabeth*. Work resumed on the *Queen Mary* in 1936 and the same year, the keel of the *Queen Elizabeth* was laid.

Meanwhile the *Rex* held both the Blue Riband and the newly-awarded Hales Trophy (awarded by British MP Harold K. Hales in 1935 for the fastest Atlantic crossing) and the French launched their Atlantic giant, the *Normandie* (with a length of 1,029 ft, the largest and fastest Atlantic liner to date) in 1933. Largely financed by the French government the *Normandie* was finally completed in 1935 and achieved a remarkable speed of 31.9 knots on sea trials. This ship was a stark departure from the upright dignity of earlier Atlantic liners: her smooth-flowing lines and steam turbo-electric propulsion repre-

The Europa *leaving the Blohm and Voss building yard. This ship was part of a massive investment to give Germany supremacy on the North Atlantic in the 1930s* (Blohm and Voss).

Left *Bridge front of the* Queen Mary (Author).

sented a revolution on the Atlantic service. The accommodation also surpassed anything seen before, with a grand hall extending to three decks in height. The in-service speed of the *Normandie* matched her appearance and on her maiden crossing from Cherbourg to New York, she averaged 29.94 knots, marginally under the magic 30 knot barrier which she exceeded on her return to Cherbourg with an average of 30.35 knots. Like many other liners before her, the *Normandie* experienced vibration problems from her powerful propellers, but when these were replaced with a new design, the problem was largely eliminated. Having soundly beaten the Germans and Italians in terms of size, speed, appearance and appointments, this magnificent French liner now had to face the challenge from the first of the British contenders, the *Queen Mary*. This event was eagerly awaited by an expectant public who looked on it not just as a question of speed, but as a contest between the traditional values represented by the

design of the *Queen Mary* and those of the brave new era represented by the *Normandie*. The *Queen Mary* finally left her building yard in 1936 after nearly six years in the making and began her trials. The speeds achieved on these trials were kept a closely guarded secret and when she began her maiden voyage on 27 May, great things were expected. However she didn't beat the *Normandie*'s time and it was another two months before she finally achieved a record crossing and gained the Blue Riband, the outward passage being completed at an average of 30.14 and the return at 30.63 knots, the first time both crossings had been made in excess of 30 knots. The *Queen Mary* was awarded the Hales Trophy, but the canny Cunard/White Star directors refused to accept it on the grounds that it implied that they were taking part in ocean racing, and this was not consistent with the company's policy of safety first! In view of the fact that the company had built a ship with the implicit purpose of breaking the Atlantic record, this is a somewhat pompous attitude, but as it turned out they would not have held the trophy for long anyway because in 1937 the *Normandie* increased her speed with a best crossing of 31.2 knots. The following year the 'non-racing' *Queen Mary* regained the record with her fastest-ever crossing of 31.69 knots.

To *Normandie* remains the distinction of being the first ship to complete a crossing in under four days, but there was little to choose between these two magnificent ships. Once again, however, Cunard managed to come out on top—

perhaps through a combination of good luck and good judgement for the *Queen Mary*, pressed into war service, held the record for the duration of the Second World War. The second of the Cunard pair, the *Queen Elizabeth*, was not completed in time to make passenger crossings before the onset of World War 2, and the war cancelled the German Norrddeutscher Lloyd Line's plans to build a superliner to be called *Viktoria* and the French Line's plans to build a companion to the *Normandie* to be called the *Bretagne*. The *Queen Elizabeth* was to make her first Atlantic crossing to New York in conditions of utmost secrecy in March 1940 and was to serve as a troopship throughout the conflict.

The Battle of the Atlantic took on a new meaning during the Second World War. Submarines and surface warships were an additional hazard for merchant ships bringing vital supplies to Europe and the carnage amongst ships and crews was far greater than anything which Atlantic weather and icebergs had inflicted in the past. Once more ships sailed the Atlantic in convoy for mutual

protection. Often sailing far to the north to escape the enemy, they found themselves running into trouble with the weather and ice. The war, like the previous world conflict, took its toll of the Atlantic liners and many other fine ships. The *Normandie* caught fire and sank in New York Harbor and was finally scrapped. The *Bremen* was damaged in an air raid in 1941 as a result of which she too was scrapped, and a similar fate overtook the *Rex*. The two Cunard Queens ran the gauntlet of many Atlantic crossings, their high speed generally keeping them out of trouble, although the *Queen Mary* did collide with an escorting cruiser HMS *Curacoa* on 2 October 1942 coming out virtually unscathed herself but slicing the cruiser in two.

The *Europa*, the *Queen Mary* and *Queen Elizabeth* survived the war and again war reparations were made: *Europa* was transferred to the French Line and operated under the name of *Liberte*. Peacetime saw the *Queen Elizabeth* make her maiden passenger voyage on the Atlantic run in 1946 but at the by-then moderately sedate pace of 28 knots.

The Cunard/White Star company made no further attempts on Atlantic records, perhaps because there was little competition but also because such affluent behaviour was not in keeping with the austere post-war times. The two 'Queens' dominated the Atlantic service, but a new rival had arisen, against which even the fastest surface crossing would seem slow. Transatlantic air transport had arrived.

Before air travel got fully into its stride, however, the Americans once more cast their eyes on the Atlantic passenger routes and under the guise of building a vessel which could double up as a troopship in wartime, heavy subsidies were contributed towards the building of the SS *United States*. Because of her military capability, information on this ship was kept secret, but it was known that she had been designed with a very high speed potential and that she was propelled by engines approaching nearly ¼ million horsepower. Slightly smaller than the 'Queens', she was built with a superstructure in aluminium to keep the overall weight down. Her full

potential was soon realized as she made her maiden voyage in 1952 in 3 days 10 hours and 40 minutes at an average speed of 35.59 knots, but such speeds and times meant little in commercial terms against those achieved by jet aircraft over the same route.

For the trans-oceanic liners the writing was on the wall and the times set by the *United States* were never to be equalled. Although the *United States* continued in service for the next seventeen years, no attempts were made to improve on her maiden voyage speeds and the ageing 'Queens' had no answer to the newer vessel. To all intents and purposes interest in Atlantic records faded with the magnificent ships which participated in them. So came to an end the long era of passenger traffic on, as opposed to above, the Atlantic. The size of the ships, their sumptuous accommodation and their speed rivalries were gradually forgotten. When national prestige is at stake normal financial considerations do not always come into the reckoning, and there is little doubt that the most magnificent liners were built to

Single-handed crossings and sailing yachts

The history of yachting as a sport and recreational pastime goes back to the seventeenth century but it was 1720 before the first recorded regatta was held. From that time on yachting developed steadily, with the size and sophistication of yachts matching the development of commercial sailing vessels. Much early yacht development was based on commercial designs, particularly pilot boats and cutters. The first yacht credited with a passage across the Atlantic Ocean was based on the design of a brigantine built in 1812. *Cleopatra's Barge* was launched off the East Coast of the USA in 1816 and was 83 ft long. There was little difference between this yacht and the commercial vessel on which it was based apart from the comfort and luxury of the accommodation and its intended purpose. In 1817 owner George Crowninshield made an Atlantic voyage, stopping off at the Azores and carrying on to cruise in the Mediterranean. The following year *Cleopatra's Barge* returned home and was sold to become a coastal packet ship, but this first Atlantic crossing founded a tradition which was to make the Atlantic one of the ultimate tests for yachts and

yachtsmen of all types, and inevitably it was not long before yachts were being specially built to make fast passages and to race across.

1850 was the peak of the packet boat era and the first commercial steamships had made their appearance on the Atlantic: this was the year when one of the most famous yachts in history, the *America*, was built. The following year this schooner crossed the Atlantic in a fast 21-day passage. The 102-ft long *America* was a true sister ship of the East Coast pilot cutters and she was built with the express purpose of sailing the Atlantic in order to participate in a series of races in England. These races round the Isle of Wight were the first in what was to become the most famous yachting event in the world, the *America's* Cup, named after the visiting yacht. *America's* success in the English races led to a rethink of British fast yacht designs, thus showing the value of international competition and the interchange of ideas.

America remained in England for many years after her initial racing success but eventually returned to the United States to be fitted out as a Confederate despatch boat and blockade

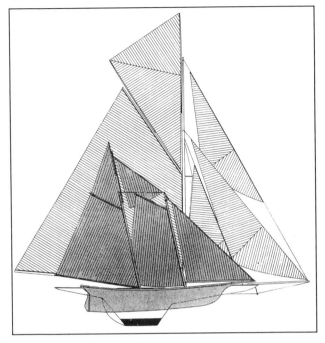

runner in the Civil War. After a long and chequered career during which she again crossed the Atlantic in 1935, this famous yacht was finally broken up, nearly a century after her launch, in 1945. *America*'s first Atlantic crossing was the catalyst for a series of similar voyages by other yachts. The *Sylvie*, which also made the crossing in 1851, took but 16 days 12 hours, but more than double that time for her return journey in 1855. Most yachts venturing out onto the oceans in this way were well equipped craft, built to the highest standards of the day and often larger than some of the commercial sailing vessels which regularly traded across the Atlantic.

Some of the larger yachts made very fast times on the Atlantic crossing. In 1866 the 107 ft-long schooner *Henrietta*

brought the time down to 13 days 22 hours. *Henrietta* had been completed just as the Civil War started. Under the command of her owner, James Gordon Bennett, she served on the government side in the war, and after this exciting period, Bennett was one of many rich young men who looked for alternative adventures. When coastal racing began to pall a race across the Atlantic was a natural outlet for this adventurous spirit. In that race of 1866 the *Henrietta* was ranged against the *Fleetwing*, owned by the Osgood brothers, George and Franklin, and the *Vesta* owned by Pierre Lorillard. All three yachts were schooners of a similar size and length and the start of the race at Sandy Hook off New York attracted a huge spectator fleet. The race was held in December,

Above left *The American yacht* Sylvie *was one of the first large yachts to cross the Atlantic in 1851.* (American Merchant Marine Museum).

Above right *James Gordon Bennett won the 1866 transatlantic yacht race in* Henrietta.

a wild time to cross the Atlantic, but chosen out of bravado to raise the stakes. Stormy Atlantic winter conditions soon took their toll of the contestants and six of *Fleetwing*'s crew were lost overboard when a wave swamped the cockpit. *Henrietta* and *Vesta* battled it out in a very close contest with the two yachts being sighted off the Scilly Isles on Christmas Eve only fifteen minutes apart—with *Vesta* in the lead. After 3,000 miles of racing this was a remarkable situation—and the finish line was at Cowes some 300 miles further on! *Henrietta* reached Cowes on the evening of Christmas Day having picked up a pilot off the Lizard, but *Vesta*, following a similar track became lost in fog on Christmas Eve and only made Cowes on

Boxing Day, having by then been overtaken by *Fleetwing* which, despite her problems, had continued to sail the course. *Henrietta* had averaged 9¼ knots over the 3,106 mile course, which compared very favourably with the times put up by the fast packet ships.

After his success in this Atlantic race, James Gordon Bennett had a new and larger schooner, the *Dauntless*, built and in 1870 this yacht raced in the second transatlantic race against the *Cambria* from Ireland to Sandy Hook. The *Cambria* was also the first challenger for the *America*'s Cup. In the westbound Atlantic race she came out on top, winning by the very narrow margin of 1 hour 17 minutes, but she lost the *America*'s Cup contest for which she had sailed over. Times across the Atlantic were much slower than *Henrietta*'s eastbound crossing, the *Cambria* taking 23 days 6 hours for the passage. Once again the Atlantic took its toll with two of the crew of *Dauntless* lost overboard. One of the conditions of the *America*'s Cup races for many years was that the challenging yacht should sail the Atlantic for the competition: the *Cambria* was the first of a long line to make this journey.

Crossing the Atlantic became a comparatively routine event for yachts of this size over the next few years. One particularly fast crossing was achieved by the 310-ton *Sappho*, with a time of 12 days 9 hours and 36 minutes between New York and Cork. *Henrietta*'s run from between Sandy Hook and Cowes, however, was slightly faster over a longer distance and remained the Atlantic yacht record for some time. In the meantime smaller craft were finding their way out onto the Atlantic. The first was the *Charter Oak* which crossed in 1856. With a length of 43 ft, there was nothing particularly remarkable about this west-to-east crossing with a three-man crew, however, for the *Charter Oak* was only marginally smaller than some of the early sailing craft which were used by colonists on the much more difficult east-to-west crossing.

However, the *Charter Oak* goes down in history as the first small yacht to make the Atlantic crossing—although her crossing time has not been recorded. A year later the slightly larger *Christopher Columbus* made the crossing from New York to Cowes in 45 days, and eight years later the sloop *Alice*, with a length

of 49 ft made a fast crossing from Boston to Cowes in nineteen days, returning the following year from Cowes to Boston and taking 34 days for the crossing. People were becoming more adventurous about the Atlantic and the idea of making crossings in really small boats started to capture the imagination. The first attempt at such a crossing was made by two Americans, Donovan and Spencer (together with a dog called Toby) who set out to cross the Atlantic in a 14 ft 6 in long dinghy called *Vision*. The boat was built in 1864 in New York and sailed on 26 June. Despite its diminutive size this craft was rigged as a brigantine with three square sails on the foremast—an extraordinarily complex rig for such a small boat. *Vision* was sighted some ninety miles off New York after two days at sea, but after that nothing further was heard: boat and crew were presumed lost at sea. Some reports put the length of this boat at 24 ft, which would seem more reasonable in terms of the rig she was carrying, and this would make her similar in size to the next small craft to make an attempt to sail across the Atlantic, the patriotically named *Red White and Blue*. This vessel was also square rigged, this time on all three masts.

The *Red White and Blue* set out to sail the Atlantic to gain publicity for a new type of lifeboat design: Ingersoll's Improved Metallic Lifeboat. With a length of 26 ft overall and a beam of 6 ft, she was fitted with watertight compartments and constructed in galvanized iron. She was quite well equipped for the crossing yet carried, as mentioned above, a full com-

The Red White and Blue *with its unlikely sail plan is given the benefit of doubt and is credited with the first Atlantic crossing by small boat in 1868* (Illustrated London News).

plement of square-rigged sails on three masts, which seems an impossibly complex rig for such a small vessel. The *Red White and Blue* left New York on the 9 July 1866 sailed by William Hudson and Frank Fitch and like the *Vision* before her, carrying a dog as well. The dog seems to be an unnecessary complication on an Atlantic crossing, but 35 days and over 3,000 miles later the *Red White and Blue* arrived at Deal in Kent.

This is a remarkably good time for an Atlantic crossing by a small boat, giving an average speed of 3.5 knots and many sceptics have doubted whether the *Red White and Blue* actually made the crossing on her own, or whether she was perhaps lifted aboard another ship for

part of the crossing, or was perhaps towed. History has given Hudson and Fitch the benefit of the doubt and the pair are credited with having made the first true 'small boat' crossing of the Atlantic.

The following year *Red White and Blue* was shown at the Paris exhibition. A Captain Gould gave exhibition at the same venue as his reason for attempting to sail the *John T. Ford* across the Atlantic. The *John T. Ford* was 22 ft 6 in long but had a generous 7 ft beam. She sailed from Baltimore on 27 June 1867, with a four-man crew which must have made this diminutive boat extremely crowded. After calling at Halifax the quartet set out across the Atlantic on the 16 July.

This was a little late in the year to get good weather in the North Atlantic and the *John T. Ford* capsized in a storm on 5 August. However, the boat was righted and continued on the voyage. She was off the south coast of Ireland on the 19 August when she was capsized once more by a huge sea. As the inside ballast fell out of the boat during this capsize, the boat kept turning over until three of the crew were overcome by exhaustion and lost overboard. One man, however, Armstrong, clung to the boat for 3½ days. Eventually he was sighted and picked up by a passing ship. The *John T. Ford* itself actually made the crossing since it was later washed ashore on the Irish coast.

This type of disaster did not dissuade other adventurers and the next voyage was another attempt to prove a new form of lifesaving craft. The *Nonpareil* was a remarkable craft for her time, being constructed from three inflatable tubes 25 ft long and 2 ft 6 in in diameter, linked together by a wooden platform. On this platform a canvas shelter was erected for the three-man crew. The *Nonpareil* was in fact a raft, fitted with two masts and schooner rigged. Crewed by three men named Mikes, Miller, and Mallene, the *Nonpareil* set out from New York on June 1868. Although the vessel and her crew experienced their fair share of bad weather, they made the crossing all the way to Southampton in 51 days. To this unlikely Atlantic craft goes the distinction of being the first inflatable craft to make the crossing. Considering the very basic standards of making airtight fabric in those days, the India rubber of the air tubes stood up very well from all reports. The *Nonpareil* was designed to be folded up and was a brave attempt to reduce the space required for lifesaving equipment on board ships. Almost certainly such craft could have saved many lives from sailing ships in trouble on the Atlantic but despite the successful proving voyage there is no record of the craft having any success in the lifesaving market.

The John T. Ford *in which four men attempted to cross the Atlantic and only one survived. The boat was washed up on the Irish coast.*

Centennial made good time across the Atlantic and was only 300 miles from fitted the dory would not be righted despite the efforts made by Johnson.

The sea anchor was still holding the boat bow on to the sea, and it was only with a superhuman effort using the motion of a big breaking wave that Johnson was able to right his craft and start baling it out, all his stores had been spoiled and he was wet through. Cold, wet, close to exhaustion, and without food, Johnson was tempted to give up the crossing when a ship hove in sight, but finding that he was only 100 miles from the Irish coast he decided to continue after being given food and water. With this news and these provisions things started to look better and Johnson continued up past Ireland into the Irish Sea and finally landed on the Welsh coast after 46 days at sea. He had originally planned to make the return crossing, but the near disaster may have made him change his mind and *Centennial* was shipped back for exhibition in the United States.

The Atlantic Ocean continued to exert a fascination for small boat sailors, much as it does today, providing a challenge for all sorts of reasons. Captain Thomas Crapo was the next small boat sailor on the Atlantic in his converted 20 ft whaleboat, *New Bedford*. Crapo and his wife crossed the Atlantic from west to east in 1877 taking 51 days from Chatham in Massachusetts to Newlyn in Cornwall. Captain Crapo had originally planned to make the crossing single-handed but then decided to take his wife along, giving Mrs Crapo the distinction of being the first woman to cross the Atlantic in a small boat. The crossing was full of incident, but the experience of Captain Crapo enabled him to cope with the crises. The boat sported a very practical Bermudan rig. Captain Crapo was later lost at sea in a little 9 ft boat named *Volunteer* in which he was trying to make a passage from Newport, Rhode Island to Cuba.

A recurring name in the history of small boat crossings of the North Atlantic is William Andrews. He made no fewer than three Atlantic crossings in small boats, the first one in 1878 when he crossed in the 19 ft centreboard sailboat *Nautilus*. Thomas Crapo's 19 ft 7 in *New Bedford* had previously been the smallest boat to make the Atlantic crossing. The *Nautilus* was specially built for the voyage by Andrews and his younger brother, Walter and the pair left Boston on 7 June 1878, completing the Atlantic crossing in 49 days. The Andrews brothers had their share of adventures but William Andrews was not deterred and he built a second boat called *Dark Secret*, only 12 ft 9 in in length. Attempts were made by American authorities to stop the proposed voyage but Andrews, this time on his own, sneaked out to sea under cover of darkness on 17 June 1888. For over two months Andrews struggled along in this tiny boat but eventually gave in when still only little more than half way across. He was picked up by a passing sailing ship.

Even this adventure didn't put him off and in 1891 he was back again, this time with a 15 ft boat which he again built himself. On hearing of Andrew's attempt, another Boston man, Si Lawlor decided to make an attempt on the Atlantic crossing also in a 15 ft boat. By the time the press got hold of these two stories they had made the event into a

Dark Secret in which William Andrews attempted an Atlantic crossing but gave up after two months at sea (Mystic Seaport Museum).

race. Widely advertised by the press, many other boats wanted to enter the race, but all were eliminated in a short trial and the pair left Boston on 21 June 1891. Lawlor's boat, the *Sea Serpent* made the crossing to Coverack in Cornwall in 45 days but once again William Andrews had to give up after a capsize and was rescued by a steamer after 61 days at sea. Thus Lawlor became the winner of the first singlehanded transatlantic race and also the credit for having made the crossing of the Atlantic in the smallest boat at that time. It was to be many years before either of these records were broken.

Lawlor was no stranger to the Atlantic having crossed the previous year in a 36 ft vessel called *Never Sink*. *Never Sink* was another potential lifeboat design and made a successful crossing from New York to Le Havre in France with a four-man crew. Lawlor was a very experienced sailor, having worked for many years on the Grand Banks and on the East Coast of the USA, and although the *Sea Serpent* was tiny she was well fitted out and his seamanship carried him safely through. *Sea Serpent* capsized during the crossing but Lawlor managed to right it and carry on. Lawlor's achievement in winning the race and crossing the Atlantic in the smallest boat ever was a remarkable performance.

Andrews was by now obsessed with the Atlantic crossing and in 1892 he was back again, intent on making the solo crossing in the smallest boat. This time his canvas-covered folding boat was 14 ft 6 in long and its construction seems totally inappropriate for such an attempt. The *Sapolio*, as she was called,

seas when a cyclonic low moved up from the Gulf of Mexico, producing conditions only marginally less violent than a full-blooded hurricane: on a small boat you probably couldn't tell the difference. 1960 saw similar severe conditions on this race which is a true ocean race covering 600 miles in sea conditions which can be made very severe if the wind is against the Gulf Stream current.

1928 saw the swansong of the large yachts in another race across the Atlantic Ocean, this time from New York to Spain. The race was for the King of Spain's Cup for the big yachts, and the Queen of Spain's Cup for smaller sailing craft. Amongst the bigger yachts, was *Atlantic*, still active after her record breaking trip on the 1905 transatlantic race. Another of the large yachts was *Elena* owned by William Bell and skippered by Charlie Barr's brother, John. The yacht was sailed by a paid crew numbering 38. *Elena* took the King's Cup whilst amongst the smaller yachts (below 60 ft in length) the victor was *Nina*.

A transatlantic race in 1931 saw few yachts over 60 ft in length and the winner was the famous Olin Stephen's design *Dorade*. *Dorade* had come third in the Bermuda Race the previous year and, sailed by the two brothers Olin and Rod Stephens, she won the transatlantic race to Plymouth in England by a margin of two full days over her closest competitor. *Dorade* followed the tough northern route favoured by *Atlantic* many years before. She went on to win the classic British Fastnet Race and the 1936 transpacific race. On *Dorade*'s

return run across the Atlantic she made the passage in the remarkably quick time of 22 days from Bishop Rock to New York.

A development of the *Dorade* design by the Stephens brothers, *Stormy Weather*, went on to win the 1935 transatlantic race from Newport to Bergen in Norway. This is a distance of over 3,000 miles with the boats tracking to the north of Scotland. This northerly track took the competing boats into the iceberg area and after taking advice from Grand Banks fisherman, skipper Rod Stephens took an inside route up the east coast of the USA and Canada and then out through the ice fields—a daring route to follow in the thick fog conditions, which gave him a well-deserved win on corrected time, coming very close to an overall win but just pipped at the finish by the 71 ft ketch *Vamarie*, some 20 ft longer than the *Stormy Weather*.

Between the wars there was another period of intense small boat activity on the Atlantic. One of the first to follow in the footsteps of William Andrews and Si Lawlor was a German, Franz Romer. He made a quite remarkable voyage crossing the Atlantic in a 21 ft canvas-covered canoe.

Romer was a Captain in the Hamburg Amerika Line and was one of the first of the single-handed Atlantic sailors who set out with a scientific objective— his being to prove that even a tiny fragile craft could survive comfortably in ocean seas. Captain Romer's craft, named *Deutsches Sport*, consisted of a wooden frame covered with waterproof canvas, a classic traditional kayak design.

Romer was virtually sealed into the small cockpit to prevent water entering the craft and he had to include enough stores on board to last the ocean crossing. Since the boat had a beam of only 3 ft, there was not much space underneath the canvas deck for all the food, water and spares required for the voyage. One of the biggest problems on this crossing must have been the inability to stand up or move around in the boat and he had to stay seated the whole time, literally for weeks on end. Even when sleeping he couldn't stretch out completely and the whole trip must have been a complete nightmare. It is a remarkable story of human endeavour. The *Deutsches Sport* was rigged as a yawl with very small sails and food and water for over three months were loaded on board. This included 55 gallons of water, 500 lb of food and a small paraffin stove with fuel. Captain Romer left Portugal and reached the Canary Islands in eleven days with a favourable wind and current. On this initial part of the voyage sea conditions were poor. Captain Romer was only able to snatch seconds of sleep between wave crests because he had to be awake and concentrate each time a wave went by to avoid capsizing. He ended up spending two seconds on watch and sleeping for three seconds. At times breaking waves crashed right over him and he reports hallucinating—which is not at all surprising!

The next stage of the journey took him from the Canary Islands to the West Indies. He set off in June and took three months on this passage, much of it without hot food after his stove caught fire and

had to be ditched. He was attacked by sharks and at night he was continually hit by flying fish. His body was covered with appalling, painful ulcers and his hair turned white. After 88 days he finally made land at St. Thomas and slept for 48 hours. He spent several weeks in hospital whilst his body recovered from the ordeal. It is amazing that Romer still found the courage to set out again to complete his voyage to New York. Starting at the beginning of October this 1,500 mile trip should have taken less than a month with favourable winds and currents, but this was the hurricane season and nothing further was heard or seen of Captain Romer and his boat. It is assumed that the boat foundered in one of the many hurricanes of that season, a sad ending for a remarkable individual.

In the three years between 1930 and 1932 an Estonian, Ahto Walter, with various crew members completed a series of five transatlantic voyages, twice in the 29 ft sloop *Ahto* and three times in its 27 ft successor, *Ahto II*. The first voyage was made from east to west, setting out in October, rather late in the season and they soon ran into a fearsome Atlantic storm which lasted for five days. Bruised and battered and with a leaking boat and a damaged rudder, they sorted out the problems and managed to make Madeira. From here they went on to the West Indies, where only three miles offshore they were becalmed for no less than fifteen days! Finally making New York they tried to enter in the 1931 transatlantic race to Plymouth but were below the minimum size. They started with the racing boats anyway. Leaks

three yachts survived the storm, but less fortunate was *Vertue XXXV* which was making an Atlantic crossing at the same time and became caught up in the same storm. *Vertue XXXV*, a 25ft sloop sailed by Humphrey Barton and Kevin O'Riordon, was hit by a freak wave and thrown on to her beam ends so violently that she was split open on the lee side of the superstructure. The vessel and crew finally made New York on 1 June 1950. Humphrey Barton ranks as one of the most experienced transatlantic sailors and has now completed twenty crossings of the Atlantic by various routes.

Despite their unpleasant experiences in this storm, the three British yachts went on to take part in both the Bermuda and the transatlantic race. In the latter race they were accompanied by two larger yachts *Gulvain* and *Carin III*. They started in July and after fine weather for the first week got mixed up in Atlantic depressions and were soon running in a full storm. Despite broaching to in this storm and losing time, *Cohoe* went on to win on handicap, but *Samuel Pepys* was the first boat home and made the fastest Atlantic crossing every achieved by a small yacht, taking 21 days and 4 hours to cover the 2,830 miles course. In the 1952 transatlantic race which again followed the Bermuda Race, *Samuel Pepys* took 25 days to cover the same distance.

1951 saw the presence centre stage of one of the smallest yachts ever to make the Atlantic crossing, the 19 ft 8 in long *Sopranino*. This lightweight centreboard yacht had been built by Patrick Ellam to demonstrate that small vessels of this type could successfully make long passages. Crewed by the famous yacht designer Colin Mudie, *Sopranino* sailed from Falmouth in September 1951 and completed the Atlantic crossing to Barbados in the highly creditable time of 37 days at sea, clearly demonstrating the seaworthiness of this lightweight concept. *Sopranino* was little more than an overgrown dinghy and the ocean voyages achieved by this boat were to have a significant impact on future ocean racing boat design by demonstrating that light weight and seaworthiness could go hand in hand.

With more and more boats sailing across the Atlantic sometimes single-handed and sometimes with full crews and with the experience of the Bermuda to Plymouth races behind them, the concept of a single-handed transatlantic race was developed by two experienced sailors, Francis Chichester and Blondie Hasler. Towards the end of November 1959 it was announced that the race was to start on 11 June 1960 from the south coast of England and finish at Sheepshead Bay in the approaches to New York. It was a tough course because prior to this event only Commander Graham had made a single-handed crossing in an east-west direction although there had been around twenty single-handed eastbound crossings. The event was to capture public imagination worldwide and also to lead eventually to the development of the modern ocean racing multihull. When the race was first announced the press billed it as the most sporting event of the century, completely

FRANCIS CHICHESTER
LIMITED
DIRECTORS FRANCIS CHICHESTER S M CHICHESTER M COOPER

9 ST. JAMES'S PLACE, LONDON, S.W.1
TEL HYDE PARK 0931   GROSVENOR 8196

NAVIGATION   SPECIALISTS
MAP MAKERS AND PUBLISHERS

25th November, 1959

To the News Editor,
(for immediate release).

SINGLEHANDED TRANSATLANTIC RACE 1960

Described by one experienced yachtsman as "The most
sporting event of the century", a transatlantic race for
single-handed sailing boats will start from the South Coast
of England on Saturday, June 11th 1960, and will finish off
Sheepshead Bay, in the approaches to New York, at least a
month later.

The race is open to boats of any nationality, size, or
type provided that they are propelled by the wind alone, and
manned by one person only. The race will be "boat for boat",
without any form of handicapping. The entries may be sponsored,
and boats need not be sailed by their owners.

The race is being run in collaboration with the Slocum
Society, a predominantly American organisation that will look
after the finishing arrangements. At least four British
yachtsmen are known to be actively preparing to enter, and it
is hoped that many more will come forward in the remaining
seven months.

The British end of the race is at present being organised
by H.G.Hasler and a committee of prospective entrants. All
enquiries should be made to Francis Chichester, 9 St. James's
Place, London, S.W.1 (Tel. HYDe Park 0931), who is temporarily
acting as Secretary to the Committee.

Add: In originating this race H.G.Hasler hopes that it may
result in simplification of gear and methods of easy handling
which will benefit yachtsmen generally.

The four firm entries to date are - H.G.Hasler,
Francis Chichester, Dr.David H. Lewis and V.N.Howells.

overlooking what had been achieved by some of the pioneers on the Atlantic.

The race, organized through the auspices of the Royal Western Yacht Club, started from Plymouth and was sponsored by the *Observer* newspaper. Four British boats entered this first race: *Eira*, a 25 ft sloop sailed by Valentine Howells; *Gypsy Moth III*, at 40 ft in length, the largest boat in the race, sailed by Francis Chichester; *Jester*, a 26 ft yacht with a Chinese lug sail, sailed by Blondie Hasler, and *Cardinal Virtue*, a 25 ft sloop similar to *Virtue XXXV*, sailed by

David Lewis. The dilemma which faced all four competitors was the route to take. The shortest route, the Great Circle route could avoid much of the adverse Gulf Stream and pick up the favourable Labrador Current on the far side of the Atlantic, but as we have seen earlier, both ice and fog are hazards on this route. The more convivial southerly routes are considerably longer in distance but are liable to attract more favourable winds. Then there is the northerly route, longer than the short Great Circle route, which has favourable cur-

Club Mediterranee, *the largest single-hander ever to cross the Atlantic.*

the benefit of modern sail-handling systems but once again the armchair pundits argued about the ability of one man to handle such a large vessel in bad weather, particularly when one of the most fancied entries, Phil Weld's 60 ft trimaran *Gulf Streamer* capsized on its way across the Atlantic to start the race. But even without this flyer there were a number of very fast multihulls entered and Eric Tabarly was back once more with *Pen Duck VI*. There was a large French entry in all classes but the media saw the race as a battle between the monohulls and the multihulls. As the yachts left Plymouth a series of deep depressions were whistling across the Atlantic, and the leaders were soon in the teeth of ferocious gales. Tabarly set the pace once more but a pack of multihulls were snapping at his heels. The gales took their toll and 51 of the entries eventually retired or sank, or had not arrived within the time limit. Colas in *Club Mediterranee* had to head into St John's, Newfoundland for repairs and once more it was Tabarly who took the

line honours again having lost his self-steering. Two entrants lost their lives on this race, the first deaths in the sixteen year history of the event, and once more there was concern about safety.

1980 saw the size of competing boats restricted to 56 ft in length. The fleet was also restricted in size to a total of 110 entries. For the first time Argos transponders were fitted to the yachts so that their positions could be checked throughout the race from the shore by means of automatic satellite interrogation. This ensured good public interest and what the yachts lacked in size they made up for in interest with an increasing number of multihulls. This time it was the turn of the Americans to sail to victory with Phil Weld bringing his *Moxie* across the finishing line in just under eighteen days to knock over 2½ days off the record set by Alain Colas. Within 24 hours of Weld finishing the race, six other boats had crossed the line—all multihulls—and from that point on it was multihulls which dominated the race. By 1984 multihulls had developed tremendously both in size and capability. The top multihulls such as *Apricot* and *Elf Aquitaine* now sported wing masts and were truly high performance racing machines. The outcome of the race was open right up until the last minute and only 21 minutes separated the two leading boats. The record set by Phil Weld was broken by the first thirteen boats in the race, two of them monohulls.

The 1984 race was also dominated by the multihulls, now permitted up to 60 ft in length. Peter Phillips in *Travacrest Seaway*, the sole British hope for an outright win, managed to hold off the pack of pursuing French multihulls right up to the final three days of the race. However sail problems slowed him down and he was eventually overtaken by Phillipe Poupon in *Fleury Michon* and

later by Marc Pajot in *Elf Aquitaine*, and Eric Tabarly in *Paul Ricard*. This was the order in which the boats finally finished but it was not the end of the story. In the middle of the Atlantic, Philippe Jentot capsized his catamaran *Credit Agricole* and fellow competitor Yvon Fauconnier had stood by for sixteen hours. Because of this delay the race committee awarded Fauconnier the time allowance and this brought him up into first place six hours ahead of *Fleury Michon* on time. Thus *Umupro Jardin V* was declared the winner of this exciting race.

The reduction in the size limit of boats and other restrictions in the 1980 race led to the French organizing their own single-handed race across the Atlantic, the *Route Du Rhum*. This race was first held in 1978 from St Malo to

The start of the 1980 single-handed race.

Above left Travacrest Seaway, *the leader of the 1984 single-handed Atlantic race until three days from the finish.*

Above right Elf Aquitaine *is typical of the modern hi-tech multihulls which take on the Atlantic today.*

Guadeloupe. Open to all-comers, the race 'followed the sun' and was perceived as less demanding but longer than the Plymouth-Newport race. After 4,000 miles of sailing the first two boats were separated by an incredible ninety seconds with the Canadian Mike Birch in his 38 ft trimaran overtaking Michel Malinovsky from France in his large monohull just miles before the finish line. Sadly the race was hit by tragedy when Alain Colas sailing *Manureva* disappeared and was never seen again. A similar tragedy occured on the 1986 *Route du Rhum* when Lois Caredec sailing the massive 85 ft trimaran *Royale* capsized and was drowned.

Safety considerations lie behind the introduction of the two-handed transatlantic race. With a crew of two at least one man could be on watch all the time, a situation increasingly required aboard the large multihulls which are prone to capsize with little warning in the event of a squall or sudden wind change. With only one man on board, the risk of collision with other vessels was also high. The first two-handed race took place in 1981 when Chay Blyth and Rob James completed the Plymouth-Newport run in just 14 days 14 hours. This record was set in *Brittany Ferries GB*, a trimaran. The second race saw 31 hours knocked off this record by Loic Caradec and Olivier Despaigne sailing the 85 ft long catamaran *Royale*.

With the success and obvious following of the single-handed and two-handed transatlantic races there have been many attempts to introduce other races across the ocean, sometimes to commemorate specific events. Such races for fully-manned boats really allow the mighty multihulls to show their paces. Races have been run from the Mediterranean to New York, from Canada to France and St Malo to New Orleans. In 1986 the largest ever yacht race across the Atlantic attracted over 200 yachts from 24 nations. This race from the Canary Islands to Barbados over a 2,700 mile route was run under strict rules to ensure that the entrants were genuine amateurs sailing cruising yachts. No damage or major injuries were reported to any of the participants and the race was won by the US entry, the 54 ft trimaran *Running Cloud*. This race is perhaps a reaction against the professionalism which has crept surreptitiously into the trans-ocean racing scene, where heavy sponsorship is required for the high performance multihulls. One of the objects of this ARC race was to bring some 'fun' back into trans-ocean racing. The fact that over 200 yachts could cross the Atlantic safely shows how commonplace this type of cruising has become.

The top echelons of Atlantic racing have increasingly become the domain of the professional. Exotic yachts, manned by fully paid crews and by skippers who, if successful, became national heroes is something of a throwback to the early days of Atlantic racing when yachts like the *Atlantic* set the pace. The traditional concept of the deep keeled, finely tuned conventional yachts has given way to a new breed of multihull ocean racers using the latest technology to produce a highly strung racing machine. Each succeeding Atlantic race, even the single-handed contests, has seen the setting of a new Atlantic sailing record. In 1986 the time was down to just over sixteen days for the east-west crossing and the two-handed races have reduced this time even further. It was inevitable that there should be interest in setting an out and out Atlantic record in the opposite direction, where the prevailing winds and currents should give the optimum conditions for a fast time.

After Alain Colas won the 1972 single-handed race in *Pen Duick IV* with a new record in the east-west direction of 20 days 13 hours, he made a record attempt on his return to France but could only achieve a crossing in nineteen days even with a full crew on board. This was a long way outside the record of just over 12 days, set nearly seventy years before by *Atlantic*. 1977 saw two more attempts, the first by Hue Long in his beautiful 25 metre maxi yacht *Ondine*. For this attempt *Ondine* was renamed *BUT* and she followed a more northerly route than *Atlantic*, just skirting the ice floes, and right up until the ninth day of the crossing she was ahead of the schedule maintained by her predecessor. Then came four days of light winds and even calms and the attempt failed by some two days. A second attempt in 1977 was made by *Great Britain III* a large 24.25 metre trimaran. Again this yacht set out with high hopes and a good forecast, but when nearing the finish there was again a period of light winds and calms which put paid to the record, although *Great Britain III* came very close with a time of 13 days 1 hour.

1978 saw Mike Birch sail the trimaran *Spirit of America*, now renamed *Chaussettes Olympia*, across. Like the others before him he had good wind conditions at the start but these tailed off towards the middle of the Atlantic and he could only manage a time of 14 days 23 hours. Part of the incentive for these attempts was a trophy donated by *The Sunday Times* newspaper, and a prize of £10,000 to the first boat to beat the record set by the *Atlantic* in 1905. It was clearly not going to be an easy record to break, but in 1980 a very determined effort was made during the *Atlantic Challenge Cup Race*—a race for fully-crewed yachts from New York to the Lizard and then on to Brest. The official distance for the Atlantic sailing record is from New York to the Lizard and this race was carefully timed to take place after the finish of the 1980 single-handed race when many of the top European boats would be in America and have to make the return journey anyway.

An unofficial entry in the 1980 single-handed race was Marc Pajot in the trimaran *Paul Ricard* and this boat had set up a good time, although nearly a day behind the leading boat. The 60 ft long *Paul Ricard* is fitted with hydrofoils which give the boat lift and enable it to sail more upright with a reduced wetted surface. For the return trip across the Atlantic, *Paul Ricard* was sailed by Eric Tabarly. Leaving New York on 22 July Tabarly sped his yacht across the Atlan-

tic to finally break the 75-year-old record with a new time of 10 days 5 hours 14 minutes. Tabarly was fortunate with his winds and his daily average speed shows a slowest of 10.5 knots and a fastest of 16.1 knots, demonstrating the sort of consistency necessary to set a new record.

By 1980 ocean sailing had really captured the imagination of the French, and large, powerful multihulls were being built under the incentive of very strong sponsorship. Marc Pajot had a new *Elf Aquitaine* and decided to make an attempt on the record following the two-handed transatlantic race in 1981. Once again the power and speed of these modern multihulls was clearly demonstrated when Pajot clipped nearly nineteen hours of Tabarly's record with a new time of 9 days 10 hours and 6½ minutes. Pajot picked up a 100,000 franc prize for this attempt and sparked off a whole series of Atlantic record attempts which brought the record down even further.

1983 saw *Club Mediterranee*, the huge 72 metre monohull which had dominated the 1976 single-handed race, back on the Atlantic again under the name of *La Vie Claire*. Skippered by Phillipe Morinay and with a sixteen-man crew this huge yacht covered the first 1,000 miles of the Atlantic crossing at an average speed of 16.25 knots. This crossing was made in February when strong winds could be anticipated and after nine days the yacht was just 145 miles from the Lizard and on schedule for the record when the wind died and the attempt failed. In 1984 in the run up

Above *Sailing* Royale *at 26 knots.*

Right *The complex electronic installation on board a modern Atlantic racing yacht.*

to the single-handed race across the Atlantic from east to west, Patrick Morvan took his 60 ft catamaran *Jet Services* to a new Atlantic record which knocked nearly eighteen hours off Marc Pajot's figures with a time of 8 days 16 hours 36 minutes. It seemed that nothing could stop the flying multihulls on the Atlantic, and 1986 saw two boats

make the attempt after that year's two-handed transatlantic race.

The two-handed race has no restrictions on length and these two boats, *Charente Maritime II* and *Royale* were both 85 ft multihulls, the largest such on the racing scene. Setting out on 11 July 1986, it was *Charente Maritime II* which set the early pace, but by the fourth day out she was overtaken by *Royale* following a more northerly route. *Royale* found consistent winds from the right direction and in a tremendous sail during which she never covered less than 322 miles in any 24-hour period, *Royale*, skippered by Loic Caradec passed the Lizard Lighthouse with a time of 7 days 21 hours 5 minutes, which was over nineteen hours inside the existing record. *Royale*'s speed on this 3,061-mile crossing averaged 16.29 knots. I had the priviledge of a short sail in *Royale* after her record attempt and the sensation of travelling at 26 knots under sail is a very exciting experience.

Consistent winds from the right direction are vital for the setting of fast times on the Atlantic. The multihulls need winds abeam or just slightly abaft the beam rather than following winds to give them maximum speed. *Royale* sported a huge wing mast the size of a jumbo jet wing, and both wing mast and hull were constructed from exotic composites to give the lightest weight and the highest strength combination. It is sad that both *Royale* and her skipper were lost in an Atlantic race at the end of 1986 but this loss serves to demonstrate the risks involved in sailing huge multihulls and the fact that you can never relax where the Atlantic is concerned. However, the record stands as a fitting memorial to Caradec, a fine seaman in the Atlantic tradition.

The summer of 1987 saw another French multihull making an attempt on the Atlantic sailing record. Phillipe Poupon left New York early in June and just 7 days, 12 hours and 50 minutes later he was passing the Lizard Lighthouse with a new record. Poupon was sailing the giant multihull *Fleury Michon* and took 8¼ hours off the record set by *Royale,* averaging 17.28 knots for the crossing. The best day's run was 520 miles to set a new 24-hour sailing record at an average speed of 21.7 knots.

One hundred years ago any small boat crossing of the Atlantic was a remarkable event and the achievement was in simply completing the crossing. Today a cruise across the Atlantic passes almost unnoticed, although for the individuals concerned it is no less a challenging and exciting experience, particularly if done single-handed. The finely-tuned multihulls which now set the sailing pace on the Atlantic appear to represent the peak of technological sailing achievement in much the same way as the last of the Atlantic liners represented the peak of marine technology in their time. Both have taken risks to achieve their high speeds and some have paid the price.

The sailing yacht has long overtaken the packet boats and clipper ships of old, but the same tough characteristics are still required from skipper and crew if a boat is to be driven hard in difficult conditions. The margin between success and failure can be very small and still requires fine judgement. Sailing craft have changed out of all recognition but perhaps in years to come the advanced multihulls of today will find themselves eclipsed by designs even faster and even more exotic.

CHAPTER 8

Rafts, rowing and unconventional craft

The role of the Atlantic Ocean as an arena for human endeavour is probably seen most clearly in the wide assortment of strange and unconventional craft which have attempted to cross it. Rowing the Atlantic must be a particularly personal endeavour, pitting one's own strength against the ocean, but some of the crossings in rafts and other assorted craft have occurred under the guise of scientific expeditions. Although some of the more adventurous crossings have been more in the nature of stunts, geared to generate the maximum publicity for the individuals involved, there has usually been an element of seriousness underlying these projects—certainly in the eyes of the participants. In many cases, however, enthusiasm has outweighed expertise. I was tempted to label these Atlantic crossings the 'freaks' but this would do many of the genuinely serious attempts an injustice, and indeed the collection of voyages listed here demonstrates the extent to which human beings will undergo long periods of suffering in order to prove their own capabilities or their point of view.

The idea of rowing a boat across the Atlantic still sounds an incredible feat and back in 1897 it must have sounded even crazier. However, it should be remembered that at that time rowing was still one of the best ways of getting around on the water in harbours, and rivers and rowing boats were in use a great deal. Out on the Grand Banks of Newfoundland rowing boats were used widely by the fishermen and often made long and epic voyages when they lost touch with their mother ships. It was this background that spawned the early small boat crossings of the Atlantic under sail. George Harbo and Frank Samuelson also had experience on the Grand Banks fisheries before they set out to cross the Atlantic by rowing.

The boat that Harbo and Samuelson used was a little 18 footer with a 5 ft beam. Built as a small whaler, it was double-ended and of clinker construction. At each end there were small enclosed watertight boxes which were intended to keep the boat afloat even if it filled with water. Otherwise the boat was a conventional open boat of the period fitted with two rowing thwarts. Harbo and Samuelson carried five pairs of oars, food and water, very basic navigation equipment and very little else.

HARBO AND SAMUELSON AND THE TINY BOAT IN WHICH THEY ROWED ACROSS THE ATLANTIC.

SLEEPING AT SEA.

CAPSIZED IN MIDOCEAN

SIGNALING A PASSING SHIP

**ROWING
THE SEA.**

Remarkable Voyage of Two
New Jersey Oyster Dredg-
ers in an Open Boat.

ACROSS THE ATLANTIC.

How They Battled Bravely for
Sixty-Two Days and
Came Out Victorious.

GEO HARBO
FRANK SAMUELSON
AND THE BOAT
FOX

10. *Richard K. Fox* was
18-ft. long and crossed
from New York to the
Scilly Islands in 55 days.
From a page in *The
New York Herald, March
21, 1897.*

The first attempt to row the Atlantic by Harbo and Samuelson in 1897.

They certainly carried no sail or mast because they didn't want to be accused of sailing the boat across. Heavily loaded in this way the boat had a freeboard of just 8 in when they set out from New York on 6 June 1897. The project was heavily sponsored by a New York newspaper and the boat was named the *Richard K. Fox* after the editor. Both men rowed during the day and at night one would sleep while the other continued rowing—a very tough watch-keeping schedule to maintain. A month out from New York the boat was capsized by a huge breaking sea, throwing both men in the water, but they hung on to handgrips built into the keel and managed to right the boat and climb back on board. During this capsize they lost a fair amount of their equipment, but they were able to pick up more provisions and water from a passing sailing ship and eventually made an accurate landfall after an otherwise uneventful crossing. They had planned to make the crossing in sixty days and in fact they completed the 3,075 miles to the Scilly Isles in 55 days—an average distance of 56 miles a day. Even though they had had favourable winds and currents which would have helped considerably, this first row across the Atlantic is an amazing feat of seamanship and endurance and deserves more credit than history has accorded it.

Another attempt at a rowing crossing was announced in 1911 by Joseph Naylor. This was to be a solo rowing attempt, but no record exists of the attempt ever having been made. Nearly seventy years elapsed before the next attempt to row the Atlantic was made by the British sailor David Johnstone who commissioned a specially designed boat from naval architect Colin Mudie. Mudie already had experience of the Atlantic having sailed across in the lightweight 21 ft *Sopranino* in 1951. He was also one of the first people to complete an Atlantic journey partly by air and partly by water. This last feat was achieved when he attempted a balloon crossing of the Atlantic from the Canary Islands in 1958. The balloon came down with 1,500 miles still to go, but the gondola of the balloon had been designed as a boat and in this the four-man crew continued the journey to Barbados under sail.

Johnstone's boat, the 15 ft 6 in *Puffin,* was built at Cowes in the Isle of Wight in cold moulded timber. A large part of the boat was enclosed to provide protection for the crew and equipment and the rowing cockpit was carefully planned to give the maximum comfort during long periods of rowing. Johnstone's crew in *Puffin* was a fellow journalist, John Hoare. Whilst this pair was finalizing plans for a departure in 1966, another Atlantic rowing attempt was being developed. Inevitably, with two attempts to row the Atlantic going on at the same time, the media hailed it as a race, thereby putting pressure on both parties and eventually, perhaps, contributing to disaster. The second pair on this Atlantic rowing 'race' was John Ridgway and Chay Blyth, both members of the Parachute Regiment and perhaps better prepared mentally for the ordeal. The boat they chose was a Yorkshire dory with a length of 20 ft and

The tracks of some of the rowing voyages across the Atlantic on the northern route.

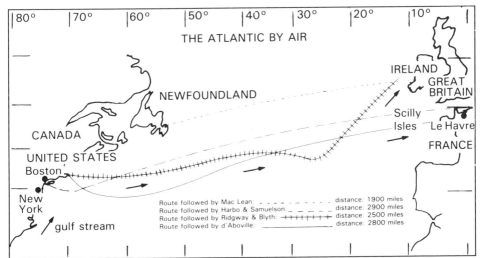

beam of 5 ft 4 in, to which turtle decks were added fore and aft to give buoyancy. The boat was strengthened and improved for its Atlantic crossing and was patriotically named *English Rose III*.

Puffin's departure point, Virginia Beach, was a lot further south than that of *English Rose III* which set out from Cape Cod. This southerly departure point was probably a mistake on the part of the two journalists for it not only considerably increased the distance they had to travel, but made it more difficult to get out into the Gulf Stream to gain any benefit from the current. *Puffin* was eventually found nearly five months after her departure, some 800 miles east of Newfoundland, upside-down and heavily encrusted with barnacles. There was no sign of her crew but the log on board continued for nearly 100 days. It is thought that the boat was overwhelmed by Hurricane Faith early in September.

English Rose III not only began her crossing from a point further north, but she also set out after *Puffin* and experienced her fair share of gale force winds

across the northern part of the Atlantic. Landfall was made on the west coast of Ireland after 92 days at sea. At one stage the crew were running desperately short of food but managed to get extra supplies from a passing ship. Ridgway and Blyth became the first people to row the Atlantic for nearly seventy years. It was an heroic effort but they took nearly forty days longer than Harbo and Samuelson and the crossing was over a shorter route.

Another epic long distance rower was not so fortunate. Bob Willis made two successful crossings of the Pacific under oars, but three times he set out to row the Atlantic, and twice he was picked up in mid-ocean. On his third attempt Willis was lost, although his boat was found empty ninety days after he set out.

The losses didn't deter others and the single-handed human-powered crossing remained to be done. The next attempt was made in 1969 when John Fairfax had a 22 ft boat built for the purpose. *Britannia I*, designed by Uffa Fox, was a double ender with raised turtle

Left Puffin, *the boat in which Johnson and Hoare attempted to row the Atlantic, but in which they lost their lives. The boat has now been restored and is in Exeter Maritime Museum.*

Right Britannia, *the boat in which John Fairfax rowed the Atlantic, spending 180 days at sea.*

back decks, designed to right the boat if it capsized. Uffa Fox's design was intended to enable the boat to be driven easily by a pair of oars and the cockpit was self-draining. A sliding rowing seat was incorporated to improve rowing efficiency and this boat was one of the best designed craft used on Atlantic rowing attempts. John Fairfax planned to row the Atlantic from east to west and had the boat shipped to the Canary Islands where he set out for his Atlantic row. There was, of course, less chance of strong winds on this southerly route and the warmer temperatures would help, but it took Fairfax 180 lonely days to make the crossing from the Canary Islands to Fort Lauderdale in Florida, which probably ranks as one of the longest of all Atlantic crossings.

This same southerly route was followed by Sidney Genders when he rowed the Atlantic in 1970. However unlike Fairfax, Genders started out from Cornwall in England and rowed from there to the Canary Islands, continuing on from the Canaries to Antigua in the West Indies, and thence on to Miami.

Genders made his voyage in the 20 ft *Khaggavisana*.

The 1960s and early 1970s saw all sorts of daring feats and publicity stunts and the Atlantic continued to be an attractive venue. A 20 ft pontoon with a single outboard motor set off from London for the USA but did not make it out of the Thames estuary. A wartime amphibious vehicle set off on a similar voyage but sank off Dover. These less-than-serious attempts echoed attempts in the 1930s to cross the Atlantic in a huge rubber ball and in two large barrels lashed together!

More seriously, Tom Maclean set out in 1969 to be the first person to row solo across the Atlantic from west to east. He chose the shortest possible distance across, leaving St John's in Newfoundland and arriving in Ireland seventy days later. The boat used by Maclean was a 20 ft Yorkshire dory very similar to that used by Ridgway and Blyth. Named *Super Silver* it had raised turtleback ends to give it a self-righting capability. Meanwhile, following his Atlantic crossing John Fairfax went on to row the Pacific in a boat called *Britannia II*, again designed by Uffa Fox. This 35 ft boat was designed for two rowers and after the successful Pacific attempt it was borrowed by Derrick King and Peter Bird who set out on a rowing attempt around the world. Leaving Gibraltar in 1974 this pair took 93 days to make the crossing to St Lucia in the West Indies but after this gruelling crossing abandoned any ideas of going on further. Another pair to cross the Atlantic on this southerly route were the brothers Geoff and Don Allum who also used the popular Yorkshire dory design and took 74 days to cross from the Canary Islands to Barbados. These adventures more or less exhausted the possibilities for Atlantic rowing but in 1980 a Frenchman, Gerard D'Aboville, set out to make the first crossing from the USA to France with oars. D'Aboville's boat, the *Capitaine Cook* was 18 ft long and had a beam of 5 ft. He covered the 2,800 miles to France from Cape Cod in just under eighty days. In 1987 Tom McLean set off on another solo Atlantic crossing and set a new rowing record across the Atlantic.

The Atlantic has seen a number of accidental and some remarkable feats of survival. One such in a small rowing boat involved two of the crew of the British tramp steamer *Anglo Saxon*, which was torpedoed in mid-Atlantic in 1940. The nearest land was the Canary Islands, 1,000 miles to the east, but the longer distance to the land to the west was chosen as the direction to steer because of the favourable currents. There were seven men in the wooden jolly boat when their ship was sunk but only two survived the harrowing seventy days at sea in this 18 ft boat. An even longer period of survival followed another sinking during World War 2. The SS *Ben Loman* was torpedoed in the Atlantic 750 miles off the Azores. One of the Chinese stewards, Poon Lim spent 133 days in a ship's lifeboat before being picked up.

There have been several attempts to cross the Atlantic by raft, although the definition of a raft is a little vague. It could be argued that the *Nonpareil*, the inflatable lifesaving device which crossed the Atlantic in 1867 was a raft, and indeed it was described by its makers as a 'lifesaving raft', but this craft was equipped with two masts and a good sailing rig whereas a raft is more usually thought of as something which drifts rather than sails. One of the first to look at a raft crossing of the Atlantic was the Canadian, Henri Beaudout. He admits to wanting to make this attempt as a means of bringing some adventure into his life, and the first raft he built, sailed by a three-man crew, left Montreal in 1954 only to be wrecked on the Newfoundland coast before getting out into the Atlantic. It had taken the crew 66 days of drifting to get to Newfoundland but, undeterred, a second raft was built in 1956 to make another attempt. Logs lashed together formed the base and a canvas-covered cabin built on the deck provided the home for the crew. A bipod mast was erected to carry a very basic square sail. This time the crew had learned their lesson and *Egare II* set out from Halifax, Nova Scotia on the 24

Three Canadians crossed the Atlantic in the Egare II *seen here after her arrival on the Eastern side of the Atlantic in 1936* (Osborne collection).

May 1956, straight out into the Atlantic. They arrived off the Lizard in England on the 20 August, having taken 87 days on the crossing. *Egare II* encountered the usual North Atlantic storms but the raft managed to weather these and even winds of over 50 knots at times.

Thor Heyerdahl achieved fame with his voyage across the Pacific on the raft *Kon Tiki*. Obsessed with trying to demonstrate the movement of early civilizations around the world, he later set out to show that there could have been a sea link between the ancient Egyptians and the early civilizations in Peru and Mexico. Heyerdahl identified what he perceived as similar advances in each society, such as the building of pyramids. The papyrus boats used by these early empires also had a strong similarity and Heyerdahl built the papyrus raft *Ra* in an attempt to demonstrate that a seaborne link could have been feasible centuries before. A great deal of research was necessary to establish the form and character of these early boats, and it was an even harder task to find people still capable of building them. The first raft of this type almost succeeded in making the Atlantic crossing, but was breaking up as it made the approach to the West Indian Islands. Later Heyerdahl built a second raft, *Ra II*, which was 39 ft long and 16 ft wide. The papyrus mattress from which this boat was constructed was 6 ft thick with raised ends. Above this a 13 ft × 9 ft cabin was constructed to provide shelter for the crew. The raft carried a bipod mast on which a square sail was rigged and both *Ra* voyages followed the favourable wind and current route down to the Canary Islands and then out across the Atlantic to the West Indies. At times the raft would travel at over 3 knots with favourable winds and currents and on the second crossing the crew experienced some big seas which the raft negotiated very well. *Ra II* finally made Barbados after a 3,270-mile journey, having taken 57 days. While this was a considerable achievement, I am not convinced that it settles the question of whether such a voyage could have been made all those years ago. It is easy to accept that a raft such as *Ra* could have been picked up by the winds and currents and blown across the Atlantic on this route with the crew being unable to make progress back to land. However, would such a boat have been equipped with provisions to enable the crew to survive on such a crossing and would a crew of such a boat have been of the calibre to establish a matching civilization on the other side of the ocean? To both questions the answer would appear to be no, and it is hard to imagine a full scale expedition being mounted from Egypt to find a new land across the ocean. Even if such a crossing had been achieved, it only seems possible for the detailed technology of a civilization to be transferred across the oceans if it was possible also to make the return journey, to inform others of the discovery. This appears to be the weak link in Heyerdahl's argument that a sea link existed, but it does not detract from the unique achievement of the crew of *Ra*.

A similar voyage was undertaken in 1976-77 by Tim Severin when he set out to demonstrate that the Irish monk St Brendan might have been one of the first discoverers of America when he made his epic voyages in Atlantic waters. As far as research can identify the Brendan voyages did not encompass the coast of America but St Brendan almost certainly reached Iceland and the Azores. The Brendan boat built by Tim Severin to try to follow the tracks of the sixth century Irish, was constructed in traditional Celtic style with a light wooden frame covered by animal skins. This comparatively light craft had a square sail hoisted on a single pole mast and was a surprisingly efficient sailing craft. Severin took the northerly route up from Ireland to the Shetland Isles and then on to the Faroes and across to Iceland then Greenland before finally making the hop across from Greenland to Newfoundland where he made his North American landfall. Perhaps even more definitively than the *Ra* voyages this replica craft proved itself capable of making an

The Brendan boat nearing the end of her transatlantic voyage in an attempt to re-enact the voyages of St Brendan (Tim Severin).

1973 and after a variety of storms and other adventures, they finally made landfall on the Mexican coastline on 20 September after a total of 101 days isolated at sea. This scientific experiment was carried out under the auspices of the *Instituto De Investigaciones and Antropologicas* in Mexico but the press degraded the whole affair by calling it the 'Mexican Love Raft.' This raft, however, had been designed by Colin Mudie who had been involved in many transatlantic craft and the fact that it made the crossing successfully is a tribute to his design. Once again sail was used to propel the raft and this was one of the few crossings of the Atlantic by this southerly route which did not stop at the barrier of islands forming the West Indies but carried on right through to the Central American mainland.

Two years later Dr Santiago Genoves, who masterminded the *Acali* experiment, conceived the idea of a further experimental raft designed with the intention of crossing the Atlantic under water. The raft designed for this had a clear plastic accommodation chamber located beneath the waterline. Once again this raft was designed by Colin Mudie and the experiment involved the study of an individual's reaction when continually surrounded by water. The whole concept was, to say the least, far fetched, and it was probably fortuitous that the raft built for this pro-

Atlantic crossing, but of course this can not prove that the same crossing was necessarily enacted back in the sixth century.

In 1963 an Atlantic crossing was made on the southerly route from the Azores to Guadeloupe in the West Indies by a Frenchman, Rene Lescombe. His 25 ft long raft was equipped with a cutter rig and although it succeeded in making the Atlantic crossing, the craft and its crew were subsequently lost at sea.

Ten years later an unusual raft voyage was enacted across the Atlantic. The voyage, aboard a strongly built steel raft, was designed to study human behaviour in a closed environment. Five couples boarded this raft, the *Acali* which set out from the Canary Islands on 12 May

ject was dropped and destroyed whilst it was being unloaded from the ship which transported it to the Canary Islands for the start of the voyage, thus ending the experiment rather abruptly.

One of the most famous scientific experiments to be carried out on the Atlantic was Dr Alain Bombard's voyage across the Atlantic in a small inflatable boat. This expedition sought to demonstrate in a highly practical way Dr Bombard's theory that a shipwrecked sailor could live for long periods off what the ocean could produce. Fish were obviously the main source of nourishment and also of liquid, although Bombard also drank limited amounts of sea water, tests having shown that sea water could be drunk in small quantities with safety. Dr Bombard's crossing ranks as an epic of survival, for Bombard existed on nothing but what was available from the ocean for 65 days. Bombard's crossing was made in a fairly standard Zodiac inflatable, 15 ft in length. It had a fabric bottom over which was a wooden slatted floor which helped to maintain the shape. Chafe was a major concern for the inflatable fabric but the boat survived the crossing with very few problems. The inflatable, called *L'Heretique*, was equipped with a small mast and sail so that Bombard could take advantage of the prevailing winds to boost his speed and the time taken is a very creditable performance. In fact Bombard started off from the Straits of Gibraltar and then stopped off at Casablanca and Las Palmas in the Canary Islands before making the long crossing to Barbados. Dr Bombard's crossing was the first in

an inflatable boat since the voyage of *Nonpareil* nearly a century earlier.

In 1978 an Irishman set out from Halifax in Nova Scotia to cross the Atlantic in an inflatable boat powered by an outboard motor and also equipped with a sail. Enda O'Coineen left harbour very quietly fearing that if his intentions were known the Coast Guard would stop him leaving. This first crossing very nearly ended in disaster, when the boat was capsized just a few hundred miles off the west coast of Ireland. O'Coineen had spent two days lashed to the bottom of the capsized boat and he was near to death when he was finally rescued by a NATO warship which was out on exercise in the area. O'Coineen had spent 79 days in the boat and vowed that he was finished with the Atlantic and inflatable boats for ever after this trip. However, he was not very happy at being remembered as the man who nearly made it across and he scheduled a second attempt to be made in 1985. The original voyage had a partly serious purpose to it, since it was intended to assist the development of a sailing life-raft which would allow survivors from a shipwreck to make progress towards land and safety. It also looked at the problems of self-sufficiency and survival at sea. O'Coineen had worked with a life-raft company developing survival equipment before this attempt but his second crossing in 1985 was intended, he said, purely to set the record straight and to get the Atlantic out of his system.

On this second attempt, O'Coineen selected a rigid inflatable for the job. This was 15 ft in length and was equip-

ped with a mast and sails as well as two outboard motors. After earlier experience on the Atlantic, this boat was fitted with self-righting equipment in the form of an airbag on a frame over the stern, which could be inflated if the boat capsized. After leaving Halifax thick fog persisted for days on end, but the *Kilcullen* motored steadily northeastwards on auto-pilot most of the time. O'Coineen encountered the tail end of Hurricane Anna but fought his way in to St Johns in Newfoundland where he stopped off for four days, filling up with 150 gallons of fuel for the Atlantic crossing. The idea was to burn off most of the fuel during the first half of the passage to get through the Labrador Current and into the Gulf Stream. From there on the sails and the current would carry the boat towards Ireland. Three days out of St Johns, *Kilcullen* encountered a storm which left O'Coineen exhausted, and the next night *Kilcullen* literally bumped into an iceberg, the inflatable tube of the boat fortunately bouncing off the berg rather than suffering damage. Another

storm as *Kilcullen* entered the Gulf Stream created further problems and two days later the boat capsized in heavy seas. Fortunately the self-righting gear worked and O'Coineen climbed back on board, shaken and exhausted. The storm raged for days and when it died away another one came up quickly. Storms continued for ten days before he had light winds and better conditions. Finally after 28 days O'Coineen made landfall in Ireland, and the voyage was over, the first rigid inflatable to cross the Atlantic.

This voyage could also claim to be the smallest powerboat crossing, but the engine was only in use for a limited amount of the time—but then so was *Savannah*'s steam engine and she is credited with the first steamship crossing. Well equipped and using modern technology, O'Coineen's voyage in a small boat on the Atlantic had tested him to the limit although the voyage only took 28 days. Consider then the sheer fortitude required by Si Lawlor and his 15 ft *Sea Serpent* on his 45 day crossing, which had featured a capsize and a desperate fight for survival in 1891.

In this look at the more unusual craft which have crossed the Atlantic, we can't miss out the windsurfers who have made the passage. In 1982 Pascal Marty made a crossing by windsurfer from Dakar in Africa to the West Indies. On this crossing Marty sailed his windsurfer all day but was taken on board an accompanying 50 ft yacht at night, where he ate and slept ready for the next day's sail. It is a remarkable effort although having the luxury and comfort of a yacht close by all the time, must certainly have made things a lot easier. It was also the French who made the first non-stop crossing by windsurfer. T. Caroni and F. Beauchene set out from New York to make the crossing to France. This crossing was made in a specially prepared tandem windsurfer which was built up so that minimal accommodation could be fitted into the hull. The crew took it in turns to squeeze through the small hatch in order to sleep and this remarkable crossing ranks with that of Captain Romer for sheer lack of space.

A windsurfer crossing in the opposite direction was made at the end of 1985 when Stefane Peyron and Bruno Pichavant made the crossing from Dakar to the West Indies. This couple

---

The Liberte *was the first windsurfer to cross the Atlantic without an escort. A two-man crew made the crossing in 1986.*

had a similar type of craft to that used on the west-east crossing and these two voyages by windsurfer certainly demonstrate the capabilities of these craft to make long voyages, even though the motivation for such trips must be a bit questionable. The Atlantic has been crossed by many strange craft and for many different reasons and I have no doubt that in the future, even stranger craft and more unusual reasons will be found for making further crossings.

Sponsorship and attendant publicity is now becoming one strong motive for carrying out unusual voyages and there will always be people whose enthusiasm will outweigh their expertise or natural caution to undertake such voyages. This motive has almost certainly lain behind some of the attempts to cross the Atlantic in tiny sailing boats. After the enthusiasm for small sailing boats towards the end of the last century, the next small boat attempt was in 1934

when Al Lastinger set out from Florida in a 10 ft sailboat. With the boat leaking badly, he only lasted a few days before he was rescued but he set out again four years later in an 18 ft vessel without achieving much more success.

In 1955, Hanns Lindemann made an Atlantic crossing from the Canary Islands to the West Indies in a 17 ft collapsible kayak, *Liberia II*. This tiny craft had a small sail to help it on its way, and the crossing took 65 days over the 3,000 mile route, thus emulating Captain Romer's remarkable feat back in 1928, although Lindemann arrived in a much better physical condition than his predecessor.

The 1960s saw several attempts to cross the Atlantic in the smallest possible sailing boat with *Sea Egg* making the crossing in 1964. This 12 ft sloop was shaped as its name suggests and was refused entry in the 1964 transatlantic race because of its size. The owner, John

American Robert Manry entering Falmouth after crossing the Atlantic in his small yacht in 1965 (Osborne collection).

Tom McClean at the helm of the 9 ft 9 in long Giltspur *in which he crossed the Atlantic in 1982* (Yachts and Yachting).

Riding decided to sail across the Atlantic anyway, and after calling at Spain and the Azores went on to Bermuda and then Panama in this tiny craft. The west-east record for the smallest boat had been held by Si Lawlor since the first single-handed crossing of the Atlantic in 1891. This record was not beaten until 1965 when an American, Robert Manry, settled from Falmouth USA, to Falmouth England in 78 days. Manry's boat was the *Tinkerbelle* which was just 13 ft in length with a 5 ft beam. Two other small craft, *Giltspur*, 9 ft 9 in in length, and *Winds Will* at 9 ft in length also sailed across the Atlantic, but the

record for the smallest has to go to *April Fool*, sailed by the American Hugo Vihlen from Casablanca to Fort Lauderdale in 1968. This amazing vessel was only ½ in under 6 ft in length. In this tiny craft, which in addition to its single mast was also equipped with an outboard motor, he took 85 days on the 3,000 mile crossing averaging just 1.4 knots.

It is hard to imagine such a record for small sizes being beaten, simply because of the sheer difficulty of living and sleeping in such a small space. However, in their quest for the daring and difficult, men do many strange things and no doubt this record will eventually be broken, but to what point it is not easy to see. Whilst many of the unusual trips across the Atlantic may have been done for the very private reason of proving something to the person concerned, living in totally cramped conditions on a tiny boat seems like a particularly odd form of masochism and one can really only feel that Atlantic crossings are done for the worst type of publicity: there is nothing to be gained technically from such an exercise, but perhaps we shouldn't be too harsh on such attempts, because with so many things now having been achieved on the Atlantic it is harder and harder to find new challenges which stretch the imagination and the physical ability of the participants. People will always find new and even more difficult ways to make the Atlantic crossing and it is perhaps a tribute to the advances in modern boat technology, that crossings by boats under 50 ft are now routine.

CHAPTER 9

Motor boats take to the Atlantic

At the beginning of the 19th century steam boats were making their faltering way out on to rivers and coastal waters, but it was over a century before the internal combustion engine made its debut as a means of propulsion on water. It provoked a change in the boating and shipping world which was to have far reaching effects. Whilst the steam engine took nearly fifty years to become an accepted and reliable motive force on the water, the gestation period of the marine internal combustion engine was much shorter, perhaps because it moved into an area where powered vessels were already widely accepted. One of the most immediate impacts of the internal combustion engine was to make much smaller powered craft a viable proposition and it was not very long before these craft started to venture out on to the oceans.

The first boat to attempt an Atlantic crossing with an internal combustion engine was the *Abbiel Abbot Low* in 1902. This crossing was made just ten years after the internal combustion engine was first fitted to a boat and clearly demonstrates the rate of development. The man behind the project was an

American, William Newman. Newman had all the right qualifications for the job, being a ship's captain and an enthusiast for the new engines. The purpose of his proposed crossing was to demonstrate that small internal combustion engines were up to the task and what better testing ground than the Atlantic. The boat was sponsored by the New

York Kerosene Company, and named after the president of this company. The *Abbiel Abbot Low* had a length of 37 ft 6 in, with a beam of 9 ft and a draft of 3 ft 6 in. The paraffin-powered engine fitted to the boat was a little 10 hp single-cylinder unit with a capacity of 150 cc. The hull of the *Abbiel Abbot Low* was built from wood, very much along traditional sailing boat lines of the day but without a deep keel. She was also equipped with sails in a ketch rig. The promoters of the voyage claimed the rig was intended to act as a steady sail in Atlantic waves but the size shows it to be very much an alternative means of propulsion. The prevailing westerly winds would certainly have helped the *Abbiel Abbot Low* quite considerably.

On an initial trial around Long Island the engine performed perfectly for nearly two days so this attractive double-ender was loaded up with fuel for the Atlantic crossing. The tanks fitted in the hull could hold 660 gallons and another seventy gallons were stowed in one-gallon cans in the engine compartment. Some 200 gallons of water were also loaded which seems a surprising amount in view of the need to carry as much fuel as possible. In case of any breakdown of the engine a complete spare engine was carried on board in spare parts, but little could be done about the transmission and propeller should they have failed. On 9 July the *Abbiel Abbot Low* with William Newman and his sixteen-year-old son on board as crew, departed from New York on their historic voyage. For six days they enjoyed good weather and covered 150 miles per day with the engine running smoothly. Then the first engine stop occurred when a blocked jet brought it to a halt. It must have been a heart-stopping moment, but the problem was soon solved and they were on their way again. Later that same day, the engine again stopped, this time with a hot bearing. This again was cured quickly, but on the seventh day despite following a southerly route to avoid the worst weather as far as possible, they encountered a storm and hove to with the sea anchor out. They tried spreading oil on the water but it had little effect. Like all

The first motor boat to cross the Atlantic, the Abeil Abbot Low, *in Falmouth after the voyage* (Osborne collection).

storms this one eventually subsided and two days later they were underway again, still in big seas. Now their problems really began in earnest with leaks from the fuel tanks: paraffin was leaking into the bilges and apart from the risk of fire, there was also the worry of running out of fuel before the trip was completed. The crew managed to seal the worst of the leaks in the tanks but they were still losing over nine gallons per day and leaked fuel had to be collected from the bilges and poured back into the tanks.

After ten days of this the Newmans were in a very bad state with the whole boat and all their clothing and bedding saturated in paraffin, but the engine, although now in need of more frequent attention, kept running. At one stage it proved necessary to take off the cylinder head to grind in the valves. On 14 August, after 37 days at sea and amidst continuing bad weather and difficult seas, the Scilly Islands were sighted off the English coast and at 6.00 pm that evening the *Abbiel Abbot Low* tied up in Falmouth habour. Although the crew were exhausted, the engine was still running well having been running for 613 hours of the 861 hours at sea. During this time the engine had consumed just under ½ gallon of paraffin an hour giving ample reserves, and an average speed of 5 knots for the crossing. There is little doubt that the sails contributed quite significantly, but this should not detract from the pioneering nature of this first motor crossing.

The next crossing by a boat with an internal combustion engine took place a year later almost to the day. The engine of the *Gjoa*, however, was fitted very much as an auxiliary and sail was the primary means of propulsion. The *Gjoa* left Christiania in Norway on 16 June 1903 under the command of a Captain Amundsen on a three-year voyage which was to see this 69 ft boat negotiate the North West Passage and finally make it way to San Francisco. Rigged as a cutter, the *Gjoa* was fitted with a Dan heavy oil motor which gave the boat a speed of 4 knots. This twin-cylinder engine was a very heavy duty unit in the style which was to become very familiar in Scandinavian fishing boats and whilst the *Gjoa* used sail when the winds were fair, the engines were used on its transatlantic crossing during periods of adverse winds or calm. While this crossing cannot be counted amongst the ranks of motor boat crossings, it certainly bears comparison with some of the pioneering Atlantic crossings by sail-assisted, steam-powered vessels.

The second attempt to cross the Atlantic in a true motor boat was also undertaken in the interests of publicity, with the objective of demonstrating that the 12 hp two-cylinder Scripps petrol engine could perform happily over long distances. The boat for this crossing was specially built for the purpose and was a very heavily constructed, double-ended hull 35 ft in length, looking very much like a conventional lifeboat design with a low waist and high ends. The boat was built for Mr W. E. Scripps who was the Commodore of the Detroit Motor Boat Club, hence the name of the boat, *Detroit*. Mr Scripps also owned the

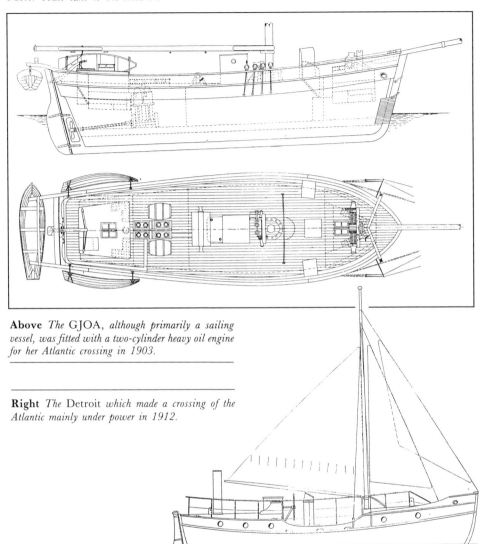

Above *The* GJOA, *although primarily a sailing vessel, was fitted with a two-cylinder heavy oil engine for her Atlantic crossing in 1903.*

Right *The* Detroit *which made a crossing of the Atlantic mainly under power in 1912.*

Scripps Motor Company, but he gave the job of skippering the boat to Thomas Flemming-Day who had crossed the Atlantic under sail the previous year. As the editor of *Rudder Magazine*, Flemming-Day could get a lot of publicity for

the project which was the name of the game as far as the engine manufacturer was concerned.

The boat was built at the Matthews Boat Company in Detroit and made a voyage under power through the Great

Lakes, the Erie Canal and the Hudson River to New York. During this trial the little 12 hp engine behaved well and preparations were made for the Atlantic crossing. Fuel was carried in five cylindrical steel tanks inside the hull. These could hold a total of 1,000 gallons and in addition there were two further 100 gallon tanks mounted on each side of the deck. A further 100 gallons were carried in five-gallon cans stowed about the boat. The whole of the centre of the boat was thus filled with fuel to supply the aft-mounted engine. For the crossing Flemming-Day enrolled three crew who had very limited experience, one of these being a paid hand as was the tradition in those days. Surprisingly there was a distinct lack of engineering experience amongst the crew but auxiliary sails were carried.

The *Detroit* left New York on 16 July 1912 and took the inside passage down Long Island Sound to Martha's Vineyard where the water tanks were topped up. Two days out into the Atlantic they discovered that the water with which they had filled up the tanks was contaminated, but they decided to carry on. This was not their only problem, because right from departure the crew had trouble with the very heavy rolling of the boat. Then the inside ballast on the boat shifted during a heavy roll and it became evident that the preparations for this voyage were less than perfect. Nine days out on the crossing the hull began to leak in the forward area, but the engine-driven bilge-pump managed to keep this leak under control. They were still having trouble with the fresh water

and they were also delayed by the fact that every day they had to stop the engine and take it out of gear in order to charge their batteries—a very poor arrangement on an ocean-voyaging boat. Crew morale was low with the constant rolling of the boat, the fact that they had to stand outside in all weathers to steer, and because the loud and continuous noise from the unsilenced exhaust added to the assault upon the senses. Heavy rolling in a small boat can be incredibly tiring, affecting eating, sleeping and maintenance work and it must have been a very weary crew who finally made a landfall at Mizzen Head in Ireland. After 23 days at sea they had crossed the Atlantic and that same evening they arrived in Queenstown to a great reception.

The *Detroit* went on to cruise up the English Channel and around the North Sea. However the return journey across the Atlantic was not attempted and the *Detroit* was eventually shipped back to the USA. Despite the problems encountered on this voyage, most of which should have been foreseen, the *Detroit* was the first petrol-engined boat to cross the Atlantic and also the smallest boat to date to make the crossing under power. The *Detroit* was fitted with stabilizing sails to try to reduce rolling, but by all accounts they seem to have had little effect in this role. The sails must have helped considerably though in maintaining speed in following winds.

Although the *Abbiel Abbot Low* and the *Detroit* were the pioneers as far as Atlantic powerboat crossings are concerned, a transatlantic race for motor boats had been proposed as early as 1904. By 1905, 34 entries had been received for this race which was to be called the 'Trans Atlantic Cup'. Amongst these was a 65 ft vessel with twin 150 hp engines built by the British Napier Company and another 65 ft craft with twin Mercedes engines. Despite the excitement and enthusiasm for the race, it was never held and as far as is known, none of the craft which were being developed to compete in it ever crossed the Atlantic. However, the boat being built by the Napier Company was very advanced for its day and its designer, the famous S. F. Edge expected his cruiser to cross the Atlantic at a speed of 17 knots to take just seven days for the crossing, a speed almost equal to that of the Atlantic liners of the time.

After initial enthusiasm, the interest in Atlantic motor boat crossings waned considerably, although in 1912 a race was run from New York to Bermuda. This race was held for several years after this date but eventually interest in it too faded and it was only in 1927 after Charles Lindbergh had flown the Atlantic in his *Spirit of St Louis* that Atlantic fever started up again.

In Britain, Betty Carstairs had a boat built to make not only a powered crossing of the Atlantic, but to set a new record, challenging the Atlantic liners. The plan developed by the builder of this boat, Sam Saunders, was to make a 3,000-mile crossing from Cowes to New York in ninety hours, maintaining an average speed of 45 knots. Saunders designed a 78 ft hull with a beam of 15 ft 6 in. The craft was to be powered by

no fewer than four Napier Lion engines developing a total of 3,600 hp. The plan was to run these in pairs alternately, stopping and starting them every hour.

The boat for this attempt, named *Jack Stripes*, had a distinctly turtleback-shaped hull with inwardly sloping sides running into a curved deck. The bow was very fine, designed to cut through the waves rather than ride over them. Four steps were incorporated into the very strong wooden hull to improve the planing efficiency. *Jack Stripes* was completed in 1928 but it never attained its hoped-for speed on trials and was eventually re-engined and used as a cruising boat. Later renamed *Voodoo*, the boat performed well in coastal races for powerboats but never made an attempt on the Atlantic record. She was perhaps some fifty years ahead of her time in both size and power.

The next record of a motor boat actually crossing the Atlantic comes in 1937 when Marin-Marie made the journey in the 42 ft *Arielle* from New York to Le Havre. Marin-Marie had already sailed the Atlantic single-handed in 1933 but with this motor boat crossing he set several new records, including the first single-handed crossing by motor boat and also the fastest crossing of the Atlantic by motor boat. *Arielle* left New York in July 1937 and took just nineteen days to make the crossing to Le Havre. The boat was powered by a 75 hp four-cylinder diesel engine and 1,500 gallons of fuel were carried. *Arielle* had a single mast on which an emergency or steadying sail could be rigged and was also equipped with a very primitive type of

auto pilot so that the boat could keep going day and night even as the helmsman slept. Marin-Marie's voyage across the Atlantic was remarkably uneventful and this is probably why it received very little publicity: it seems to be disaster or near disaster which captures the public's imagination.

In 1939, the first motor boat crossing from east to west was made in a 31 ft boat named *Eckero*. Like the *Gjoa* 35 years before, the *Eckero* sailed from Scandinavia. The reason for the voyage was an unusual one. The owner, Uno Ekblom, was unable to obtain a US visa and so couldn't buy a steamship ticket; he therefore decided to make the crossing in his motor boat. Eckblom had built the *Eckero* some ten years previously and it was fitted with a single-cylinder 10 hp diesel engine. The trip from the Baltic was a good proving run and the final departure on the Atlantic crossing was made from Falmouth on 9 June 1938, heading down for the Azores where landfall was made after a 1,250 mile pasage in 9½ days. After a day resting and refuelling, the *Eckero* set off for Bermuda 1,800 miles away. The three-man crew arrived on 7 July and again after a day refuelling and resting, made the final crossing to New York where they arrived having completed the 3,752 miles crossing in 34 days. Like the voyage of the *Arielle* this trip was notable for its lack of incident and again received very little publicity, perhaps partly due to more important concerns on the world stage.

After the war, powerboat crossings were resumed. The 52 ft converted lifeboat *Aries* left England in 1955 and made a double crossing of the Atlantic, arriving in New York on 26 May and returning to Darmouth by 6 August. On this, the first double voyage by a motor boat, bad weather was experienced in both directions but the solid lifeboat design enabled the boat to sail through without problems. A similar voyage was made by the sturdy motor fishing vessel yacht *Kytra* in 1963, but this yacht stayed in America over the winter and returned the following year.

As engines became more reliable and technology improved, crossing the Atlantic by powerboat became more common. In 1958 an attempt to make an Atlantic crossing was made by a tiny 22 ft motor boat powered by twin outboards. Like previous vessels the objective was to promote both the boat and the engines, this time in the pleasure market. The boat, *Coronet Explorer*, was a standard 22 ft fibreglass design produced by Coronet Boats in Denmark. The owner of the company, Aole Botved, was accompanied by American Jim Wynne, a boat designer who was to achieve fame in nautical circles by inventing the first modern stern drive unit. For the 1958 crossing the boat was powered by twin 50 hp Johnson outboards, and the plan was to make the Atlantic crossing in company with a freighter the *Clary Thorden* from which the diminutive boat could receive fuel twice a day. This meant that the *Coronet Explorer* had to keep with the freighter which was not inclined to delay its voyage unneccessarily.

The *Coronet Explorer* set out from Copenhagen heading north-about round the top of Scotland. In the passage between the Orkney and Shetland Islands, bad weather was encountered and the tiny boat experienced such a rough ride that eventually it had to be lifted on board the freighter until the weather eased some sixteen hours later. The boat was then put back into the water and the voyage continued. The engines suffered continual problems from spark plug fouling but the voyage continued until bad weather was again encountered off the coast of Nova Scotia and once more the tiny craft was lifted aboard the freighter. Approaching the US coast the boat was put back into the water, and finally after 10 days 16 hours 18 minutes, the *Coronet Explorer* arrived in Newport. Of the 3,433 miles covered by the freighter, the *Coronet Explorer* had covered 2,986 under her own power. This was the first crossing by an outboard-powered boat, although the freighter's assistance renders it less than a true Atlantic crossing.

In 1957 the *Dana Rescuer*, a new life-boat concept, made a powered passage across the Atlantic. It was the owners' original intention to make a complete single-handed circumnavigation of the world by powerboat and this tiny 23 ft metal craft set out from the Danish port of Esbjerg, calling at England before setting off on the Atlantic crossing. Several stops were made on the way, the *Dana Rescuer* taking the southern trade wind route via the Canary Islands and the Cape Verde Islands before completing a 33-day passage to Panama. The *Dana Rescuer* was powered by a Perkins 46 hp diesel engine and is reputed to have had a range of 4,000 miles at an average speed of 6 knots, although there may be some doubt about this because of the frequent stops at ports on the way. The *Dana Rescuer* was well equipped for ocean passages with the cockpit fully enclosed by a perspex window and the boat being capable of self-righting in true lifeboat style. A sail was fitted to harness the

power of the wind when it was abaft the beam. Although she successfully made an Atlantic crossing the *Dana Rescuer* went aground in the Americas and was prevented from achieving the distinction of circumnavigation.

1977 saw a new concept of Atlantic crossings develop. For 25 years the SS *United States* had held the out and out record for the Atlantic crossing at 35.5 knots but now a daring attempt was to be made to challenge this long standing record by a powerboat only 40 ft in length. By this time offshore powerboat racing was a well-developed sport to the degree that boats were capable of speeds up to 60 knots. In 1974 Dr Bob Magoon had set a record for a run up the eastern seaboard of the United states from Miami to New York at an average speed of 55.4 mph. The boat used for this record attempt was a 40 ft Cigarette deep 'V' hull powered by twin 450 hp Mercruiser petrol engines driving through Mercruiser stern drive units. The 55

Right *Bob Magoon's* Citycorp Traveller *in which he set out to break the Atlantic record held by the* SS *United States.*

Far right *The crew of* Citycorp Traveller, *Jack Greenburg (left), Rick Lamore (centre), and Bob Magoon.*

mph average was a remarkable achievement on this 1,257-mile run because the boat had a top speed of just over 60 mph. One refuelling stop was made at Morehead City in North Carolina and both stern drive units were also changed: this trip took 22 hours and 41 minutes.

The success of this journey demonstrted to many people the ability of a boat of this type to undertake long voyages at high speed provided the refuelling could be organized, and this led Bob Magoon to look at the possibilities of a trans-ocean crossing. It was initially proposed to do a complete round-the-world trip, but when one of the promoters pulled out, Magoon decided to tackle the Atlantic speed record held by the SS *United States*. With the help of Roger Penske the project was put in hand and the American financial institution Citycorp agreed to sponsor the project. Also helping out was Mercury Marine with whose assistance the boat was powered by four 200 hp Mercury outboard motors. The boat chosen for the Atlantic crossing was a 36 ft Cigarette, a well proven hull widely used in offshore racing and the boat was fitted with tanks to hold 1,610 US gallons of fuel.

The plan called for a start from Rota on the south coast of Spain but to make the actual departure point for the record run at Cape St Vincent which is the westernmost land point in Europe. Three fuel stops were scheduled on this Atlantic crossing, the first two in the Azores and a final one in mid-ocean. The first Azores stop would be at Sao Miguel Island after 915 miles and the second at Flores, 360 miles further on and the westernmost island in the Azores group. The final fuel stop would be a ship in mid-Atlantic, equally distant from Flores and the finish line at the Nantucket Lightship. The three-man crew comprised Magoon (as skipper), Jack Greenberg (as navigator) and Rick LaMore as mechanic. Aircraft would monitor the voyage as much as possible,

flying overhead and acting as a communications link. The *Citycorp Traveller* was equipped with the latest electronics available, including Omega and satellite navigation. It was planned to make the crossing in three days, but there was nowhere to sleep comfortably on board and the crew were accommodated in individual padded compartments in the cockpit. A small wheelhouse gave some protection from the elements but it was a hard, tough ride.

Once a suitable weather forecast had been received the *Citycorp Traveller* set out in early morning to get the advantage of maximum daylight on the first day's run. After only a short distance, however, the boat encountered heavy seas off the south coast of Portugal and was slowed considerably. More worryingly it used up more fuel than expected, but the crew pressed on, averaging 40 knots right through the night. Early the next morning they found themselves just 120 miles from the first refuelling stop in the Azores, but with fuel for only fifty miles left in the tank. Attempts were made over the radio link to get a boat to come out from the Azores with additional supplies, but in the meantime a large tanker had been sighted and flares were fired to attract its attention. The tanker stopped and the crew climbed on board to try and get some fuel. Ironically, although the tanker was loaded with crude oil there was no suitable petrol on board, so she towed the *Citycorp Traveller* for ninety miles until it was within range of the Azores with the little fuel remaining. By this time the weather was fine and the crew had no problem in making the final run into Sao Miguel. Here a council of war was held because, despite the delays, there was still the possibility of *Citycorp Traveller* breaking the record. However, the fact that the boat had been towed by the tanker ruled out any possibility of claiming the record and it was decided to abandon the attempt.

Magoon was not someone to give up easily and in 1978 he put together another project to try and wrest this longstanding record from the *United States*. The same route was selected for this second attempt but it was planned to use a larger boat, this time a 45 ft Cigarette hull powered by no fewer than six 200 hp Mercury outboard engines. This boat would carry 2,500 US gallons of fuel and the same refuelling stops were planned. This record attempt too was abandoned because the crew experienced trouble during trials in getting all six of the outboard engines to run properly, the two outboard engines not getting adequate water to the propellers. When the postponement was announced it was planned to just put the project back for a year, but in fact it led to the abandonment of this particular project when Mercury Marine pulled out its support.

In 1979 Magoon started work using the same hull but this time using two diesel engines each of 1,100 hp. These twelve-cylinder General Motors diesels had been specially developed by Roger Penske and were linked to Arneson drive units with surface propellers. Development work on this boat took some time but when it was finally tuned up it had a speed potential of 70 mph when light on fuel, and even with its full fuel load of 14,000 lb (equivalent to nearly 2,000 US gallons) this boat would still do 50 mph. In 1983 Magoon used this boat to make an attempt on his own Miami/New York record, but the boat suffered gearbox problems and also encountered large seas forcing the record attempt to be abandoned at North Carolina when they put in to refuel. Magoon had set up this boat to attempt the Atlantic record but was forced to abandon the idea and since no sponsor could be found the record set by the SS *United States* remained unscathed.

In 1977 a fifty-year-old American, Alan Cargile, planned to make an Atlantic crossing in a powerboat to commemorate the fiftieth anniversary of the aircraft crossing by the *Spirit of St Louis*. For this trip he selected a 30 ft Great Lakes cruiser, which certainly looked most unsuitable for ocean crossings with its large areas of glass and its shallow draft. The *Spirit of Nashville*, powered by a single Volvo Penta diesel engine linked to a stern drive unit, was more of a houseboat than an ocean-going vessel. When Cargile left New York with two companions on 16 July 1977, the boat was loaded with nearly four tons of fuel. Speed was kept down to about 6 knots to minimize fuel consumption, but after five days, having covered about 1,100 miles, *Spirit of Nashville* ran into a storm with waves reported to be over 30 ft in height. Lying to a sea anchor and keeping the engine in reverse they managed to survive this storm, but the radio had been put out of action and they went into St Johns in Newfoundland for repairs.

After five days they set out again and encountered another storm which again put the radio out of action, but this time they carried on and arrived at Le Havre on 14 August having taken 31 days for the crossing. The engine had run non-stop for 695 hours to give a fuel consumption of 2.13 gallons per hour. This was proof of the capabilities of modern small boat diesel engines and Volvo Penta achieved a great deal of positive publicity from the voyage.

Rival marine diesel engine manufacturer BMW recognized the value of Atlantic crossings in promoting its products and agreed to support an Atlantic double crossing planned by a French boatbuilder, META. The boat for this event, the *Voyageur 47* was a modern sailing yacht type hull, 47 ft long, designed to offer minimum water resistance and thus minimize the power necessary to propel it through the water. This hull design was developed in conjunction with naval architect Michel Joubert, and it was fitted with fuel tanks to give a total capacity of 1,850 US gallons for the Atlantic crossing. Twin BMW D50-2 diesels produced 45 hp at 3,000 rpm. These engines gave the aluminium hulled boat a top speed of 9.5 knots and an economical cruising speed of 7.2 knots. The route chosen for this crossing was from Lyon on the River Rhone, where the boat was built, to New York. This meant proceeding down the River Rhone to Marseilles, then across the Mediterranean to Gibraltar, and from there to Madeira, Bermuda and on to New York. The return journey would substitute the Azores for Madeira to keep the boat on a more northerly track to take advantage of the currents. During the crossing the other main sponsors of the trip, Elf Equitaine, set up a small laboratory on board to allow testing of the engine oil and fuel.

The crossing from Lyon to New York was made non-stop without incident and this east-west passage was claimed to be the first such made by a small powerboat (earlier voyages had been made with stops en route). *Voyageur* covered 4,800 nautical miles non-stop in just 720 hours and for this distance used only 5,000 litres of fuel, so it ranks as one of the most fuel-efficient and probably the longest non-stop voyage ever made by a powerboat.

Although powerboats now make Atlantic crossings each year, such a passage will always require a degree of planning. Using the optimum route, there are still at least 1,200 miles to cover without refuelling. An Atlantic crossing by motor boat at slow speed is not a difficult proposition any longer, although there will always remain the weather to contend with and any motor boat attempting the passage must be completely seaworthy.

Voyageur Elf Marine *seen here leaving Lyon at the start of its non-stop Atlantic crossing to New York.*

The appropriately named Half Safe *in a calm in mid-Atlantic.*

'Seaworthy' is hardly a word which could be used to describe *Half Safe*. This wartime-built amphibious craft was designed for river crossings in fine conditions. American Ben Carlin and his wife set out to cross the Atlantic in this vessel and, quite amazingly, succeeded! As Ben Carlin describes it: 'These Ford amphibious quarter-ton trucks proved almost useless in military service. With a freeboard of 12 to 15 in unladen, they were easily swamped in all but the calmest of inland waters.' Carlin was not a man to be put off easily and he converted the craft by building a cabin on the top, creating bow and belly fuel tanks and generally adapting the craft in every way he could to make it more suitable for an ocean crossing. The couple sailed from Halifax in Nova Scotia in 1950 and after stopping in the Azores and Canary Islands, *Half Safe* made a landfall at Cape Juby on the African coast and then continued the voyage by land up into Europe. *Half Safe* survived some extremely bad weather which was severe enough to test far more seaworthy craft and also experienced mechanical and fuel troubles but Ben and Elinore Carlin triumphed.

High speed crossings such as that attempted by Bob Magoon enable the weather to be predicted with a degree of accuracy over the whole route, but even when it is in a comparatively calm mood the Atlantic Ocean can throw up some uncomfortable seas for a boat travelling at 40 knots or more. At these speeds even small waves can make for an uncomfortable ride. The Atlantic does not give up its secrets easily, but Magoon's high speed attempts created a lot of interest amongst people involved with fast powerboats. The absolute Atlantic speed record had stayed still for too many years, and with the Atlantic liners never being likely to attain high speeds again, several people started to look very seriously at their chances of taking the record with a variety of schemes. It remained one of the last big challenges on the Atlantic. By 1984 the Atlantic had not even been crossed by powerboat at planing speeds which start at around 18 knots, let alone at the magic 40 knot figure which Bob Magoon was aiming for. There was a lot of work to be done but the challenge was there and it was not long before it was taken up.

The challenge to the liners mounts

Magoon's boat was little more than an offshore racing boat, specially adapted to take on the oceans: although his attempt failed, it demonstrated that there was a distinct possibility that a boat of this type could set a new Atlantic record. The Atlantic offered the ultimate testing ground for new powerboat concepts. When catamarans appeared on the offshore power racing scene, the builders saw the Atlantic crossing as a way to prove that their fast boats were more than 'fair weather sailors'.

Clive Curtis and the late James Beard were the designers of the first catamarans to be used in offshore powerboat racing. Developed from circuit racing designs, these craft soon proved themselves in open sea conditions, but Curtis and Beard, running a company called Cougar Marine, were looking for greater things: they wanted to convince potential buyers that such craft were equally suited for work as fast patrol boats or passenger ferries. A high speed crossing of the Atlantic would be just the right way to convince any doubters, and the seeds for the idea of a new record attempt were sown. Designing a suitable boat was only a small part of the exercise: compromises between the weight of the fuel, the power of the engines and the size of the boat were finely balanced against the speed, but it looked as if it might be possible.

Cougar were looking at the traditional Atlantic record from the Ambrose Light Tower to the Bishop Rock rather than the southerly route favoured by Magoon, but mid-ocean refuelling, the navigation of such a craft, driving the boat at high speed day and night, and the problem of trying to keep the crew alert for three days when suffering tremendous punishment from the movement of the boat were problems that had to be overcome. Great advances in weather forecasting implied that it would be possible to predict the weather for a three-day crossing to a reasonable degree of accuracy. Then there was the question of raising the money, since the project looked as if it could cost over £1 million. As they went deeper and deeper into the project the problems often appeared to be insurmountable, and yet gradually they were resolved and the project took shape.

When the Toleman Group purchased a controlling interest in Cougar

Marine in 1980, they inherited this transatlantic project. Ted Toleman, with his background of motor racing, was not one to resist a challenge, and he had the plans dusted off and the project resurrected. In addition to the hard commercial motives for the project, Toleman was also fired by a sense of national pride, hence the name for the projected boat, *Spirit of Britain*. The early ideas for this venture were based on a 58 ft catamaran, powered by twin Rolls-Royce diesels. This would make the project an all-British affair. Disc jockey Noel Edmonds and experienced seamen Jock Wishart, Tim Ridgeway and Tim Powell were involved in the project. Whilst the search for sponsors started, Toleman gave the go-ahead for Cougar to build an aluminium prototype at the company's newly established yard in Miami, and this served as a test bed for ideas for the future transatlantic boat.

In the early planning stages mid-ocean refuelling appeared to offer the greatest problem. It looked as if three stops would be necessary, and on the northern route they would all have to be from ships, one of them in mid-ocean. Then it began to look as if a 58 ft vessel was too small and it was back to the drawing board to look at a larger design. This in turn meant that the Rolls-Royce engines would not be suitable and the West German company MTU came on to the scene. Gradually the design of a sleek 65-footer emerged, just big enough to squeeze two 2,000 hp V12 diesels into the twin hulls, and the project moved forward another step. There had been a lot of support for this project from

industry with numerous offers of equipment, but with the project now costed at around £1.5 million there was still a big gap in funding to overcome, and the search for a major sponsor started. By mid 1984, Toleman had made a firm commitment to this project by sanctioning the construction of a 65 ft boat at the Cougar works to make a challenge possible in the summer of 1985—a brave decision without the major funding necessary to follow the project through. As work on the boat started, the team for this new project was assembled.

Steve Ridgway from Cougar Marine was appointed Project Director and both the Royal Navy and the Royal Marines promised co-operation in various aspects of the project. Chay Blyth was involved with the original prroject and came into this new team, whilst I joined the team in October of 1984 as navigator. Experience of ocean navigation on board ships and of high speed navigation on offshore racing boats gave me the right background for this job, and the search for the right electronic equipment to install in the boat began. Early on we made the decision to rely almost entirely on electronics for navigation, simply because at the speed we were going to be travelling, conventional navigation techniques would be very difficult. On a high speed boat there is no question of standing on the deck with a sextant in your hand as the navigators of the old liners had done. Having made the decision to go electronic, we then had to look at an inventory of equipment which would not only do the job adequately but which would

end, so that the deck could be completed. This was our first real glimpse of the boat in which we were to trust ourselves for 3 ½ days on the Atlantic, and whilst it looked huge as it emerged from the building shed, I think we were all conscious that day that it would look tiny out on the lonely waters of the Atlantic.

On a grey day at the end of December the hull was brought out once more, this time to make the short journey to Littlehampton harbour where it was to get its first taste of salt water. Launched into the river, the hull was towed round to the Cougar yard at Hamble, where the fitting out was to be done. Now we could really get our teeth into the planning and plotting of the crossing, but a lot of what we were doing was speculation because nobody had crossed the Atlantic at such speeds in a boat of this relatively small size. Nobody had spent three days or more cooped up in a small high speed craft as it pounded across the oceans, and nobody had much experience of driving high speed craft at night in the open ocean. It all sounded pretty dangerous when considered in the cold light of day and we were constantly coming up with potential problems and possible solutions. It was an exciting time and the project team gradually welded itself together into a cohesive unit, but the spectre of sponsorship still hung over the project. However, by early January, the Virgin Atlantic Airline was looking decidedly interested

give us a measure of redundancy should any of the instruments fail during the crossing.

The first metal was cut for the hull in September 1984 but sadly not before James Beard, who had conceived this Atlantic project, died of leukaemia. He would have approved of the sleek aluminium craft which gradually took shape in the Littlehampton building shed under the watchful eyes of the Cougar crew. Finally, on a brilliant sunny December day, the main hull section emerged upside down from the building shed to be turned over end for

in supporting the project and this is where the Richard Branson style had a fairly sudden and dramatic impact on the whole project.

Virgin Atlantic's involvement gave the opportunity to make an announcement to the press and Cougar Marine too were keen to get as much publicity as possible for its boats. Early in February, 400 members of the world's press assembled at Gatwick airport, complete with passports, to board Virgin Atlantic's 747 jumbo jet. The project was announced as the aircraft flew in low circles over the Bishop Rock Lighthouse, causing a minor panic in the Scilly Isles as residents thought the aircraft was in trouble, but the press was duly impressed and the world now knew what we were up to. Our lives were never to be quite the same again. This press launch was my first meeting with Richard Branson, the boss of the Virgin Group which encompasses records, films, videos, clubs and of course the airline. His was a style which was going to dominate the project over the next eight months as day by day *Virgin Atlantic Challenger*, as the boat was now called, grew into a potential record breaker. Branson while apparently casual and impulsive, almost schoolboyish in his approach to things, had a very different style from Toleman who was a precise, careful man. The two worked together reasonably well on the project, but one could often sense an underlying conflict in approach which might flare up into a major problem. Fortunately the leaders of the two camps involved in the project, Virgin Atlantic and Cougar, were not involved in the day to day organization which was largely in the hands of Steve Ridgway, with growing back-up from Virgin personnel such as Rod Vickery, whilst from the Toleman side, PR man Chris Moss and Chris Witty came into the project. Nobby Clarke joined us from the Royal Navy as the on-board engineer, backed up by Pete Downie who was doing much of the fitting out work on the engines, using his vast offshore racing experience. Agreement had been reached with the BBC to produce a documentary film of the project, so this meant that our footsteps were continually dogged by the *Tomorrow's World* film crew, and Peter McCann, a *Tomorrow's World* presenter, was designated to join the crew. Two Royal Marines were being selected to join the crew as divers, for propeller changes and also to help with the refuelling.

There were many problems both large and small to resolve. Refuelling in mid-ocean remained one of the most difficult since we had to find ships to do the job. The whole project would hang on the weather conditions in the Atlantic, and we had to organize detailed weather reports too. Here the Meteorological Office at Bracknell, as well as specialist companies such as Noble Denton in London and McLaren Plan Search in Halifax, were enlisted. Then the route had to be planned and plotted in detail, and I spent hours with the Atlantic charts trying to determine the best track, taking into account all the many variables such as fog and icebergs and even the shallow water on the Nantucket Shoals—the same dangers which had faced Atlantic

on short trips around the Isle of Wight and across the English Channel, but the trials culminated in a 1,000-mile test run which took *Virgin Atlantic Challenger* down the English Channel and out to get a taste of Atlantic waters for the first time. Driving the boat hard through the night on this trial gave the crew their first sobering taste of what the crossing conditions might be like and on the return run into the English coast, a trial landfall was made at the Bishop Rock Lighthouse. Further on up into the English Channel, a rendezvous was made with a refuelling ship to test out the refuelling systems on a practical exercise and all this experience gave us more confidence in our ability to face the rigours of the Atlantic crossing. The trial showed just how tough the real thing was going to be: 3,000 miles is a long way and it was a thoughtful crew which continued its physical and mental prepartions whilst arrangements were made for the boat to be shipped to the USA.

A nine-man crew had been selected for the Atlantic crossing and they were all on board when *Virgin Atlantic Challenger* left her building yard for the final time on the way round to Liverpool for shipping to the USA. It was midnight when the boat left and a small crowd of well wishers assembled to see the boat depart. I think that at this stage all the crew were conscious of the responsibility on their shoulders and the daunting task ahead. The journey round to Liverpool was not without incident. Twice the mighty engines cut out as problems developed with the electronic controls system. However, Liverpool was reached on schedule after a 400-mile trip, and the next we saw of the boat was when she was being off-loaded in New York.

New York put on a great show for *Virgin Atlantic Challenger* with reception parties and great demonstrations of enthusiasm. We settled into the Ryetown Hilton Hotel, north of New York City and close by the base selected for the boat at Mamaroneck. There was still quite a bit of work to do on the boat to get her ready to face the Atlantic and whilst this was going on the weather charts started to come in from England and Canada. The refuelling stations in the Atlantic were put on standby and Esso, who were supplying the fuel and helping with the organization of the refuelling, gave us every co-operation. The only thing that wasn't co-operating at this stage was the weather. Day after day we would meet to study the charts as they came in and day after day the depressions moving across the North Atlantic right on our track would maintain their monotonous progress. At times the weather conditions seemed to improve, but when it opened out at one end it seemed to close in at the other, and after weeks of waiting we began to despair about ever getting the conditions we sought. There was one time when it looked distinctly hopeful and we put everybody on 24-hour alert, only to stand everything down again after twelve hours when the next forecast didn't confirm the expected clearance. At high speed experience had shown that waves over about 6 ft in height would slow the boat and we were beginning to appreciate that the Atlantic plays to its own tune when it comes to wind and seas, even in the summer months.

During this period of waiting, we frequently thought about all the other people who had been out on the Atlantic on different attempts for records or just out to make the crossing. Although our top speed exceeded that of the liners, we were much closer to the wind and water than their cosseted passengers. Then there were the lonely single-handers who had no sophisticated forecasting services at their fingertips, who had to rely on their seaman's instinct to get them across. Whilst our challenge was different from the others in form, we were joining a select band of explorers, traders and adventurers who had taken on the Atlantic in many different ways and who must have suffered similar apprehension before starting off. We began to realize that it was a tall order to get suitable conditions over 3,000 miles of the world's most unpredictable and stormy ocean. The fog and ice which we could expect by following the Great Circle route were things we would have to live with, but what we desperately needed were reasonably calm seas and moderate winds.

July passed with no break in the weather monotony and then, after what seemed like an interminable wait of nearly six weeks, the weather relented. It did not grant the relatively calm, gentle conditions which we had hoped for, but it appeared to be within our margins of safety and offered us a chance which we decided to take. In the early hours of 10 August, we roared down the East River for a final farewell to the world's press and television, and then it was out under the Verrazano Narrows Bridge to the Ambrose Light Tower following a route ploughed by many Atlantic hopefuls in the past. At the Ambrose Light the timekeepers gave us the countdown, and at 6.30 am local time, we roared across the start line— our own Atlantic record attempt was on its way at last. As we headed up the coast of Long Island towards the Nantucket Shoals we made contact with the control centre in London via Portishead Radio. This was to be the start of regular contact with our control centre which was not only handling all the press enquiries, but also keeping a careful check on our progress and providing the essential back-up. Conditions on this first leg were not too bad although there were some uncomfortable seas. We were running at around 44 knots and we had four hours to settle down into a watchkeeping routine within the tight confines of the wheelhouse and cabin before the first real challenge of navigating the Nantucket Shoals.

The route selected here was close in land round Nantucket Island through narrow unmarked channels, this being the shortest route, but at times we were in a mere 12 ft of water. This was where the electronic systems really helped, with the Loran position finding systems linking up with the electronic chart: twenty miles of negotiating these narrow channels and we were then out into the more open waters of the Atlantic, heading up over the George's Bank. The miles were slipping by in a satisfying manner but

the wind had freshened from the northwest, as predicted, to give the boat an uncomfortable motion as we closed the coast of Nova Scotia.

Although the sea was on our side the fog certainly wasn't, and from Cape Sable onwards we had that to contend with. This required intense concentration on the two radar displays and the first real fright came when over 100 targets appeared ahead on the three-mile radar range. It looked like measles on the radar screen, but in fact these targets turned out to be fishing buoys with radar reflectors. It was nevertheless an anxious moment as we rushed towards them at over 40 knots. The engines were performing well and we settled down into the routine of the crossing. After twelve hours running we made rendezvous with the first refuelling ship, a small Esso tanker which had come out from Halifax. The rendezvous was made right on schedule and in the correct place. We tied up alongside, hoses were passed across and in under half an hour we had

loaded what we thought was a full fuel load and were on our way into the darkening skies of the Atlantic night. Our course from Halifax was to take us up close under Cape Race, the southeast corner of Newfoundland and then out over the Grand Banks to the second refuelling stop in the Flemish Pass. Fog continued to be a problem right through this long night and as we approached Cape Race we were entering the area where we might expect to find icebergs. The planned route took us within a mile of Cape Race, and by going into shallow water in this area we hoped to pass inside any icebergs which might have congregated off the headland. By dawn the next morning Cape Race loomed up out of the fog, dark and threatening, but we were still on schedule and the weather conditions were still allowing us to keep up a good speed, although the continual jolting motion which we had been experiencing for 24 hours now was becoming very tiring.

With 1,000 miles behind us we still

had the bulk of the Atlantic ahead, and as we headed out from Cape Race there was growing concern about our fuel situation. Thinking we had loaded the full 10 ½ tonnes of fuel we should have had sufficient to cover the distance to the next refuelling stop, but checks of the fuel in the tanks showed that we would run out of fuel whilst still fifty miles from the ship. What had gone wrong? We looked at all the possibilities, and the only one that seemed to fit the bill was that in filling the tanks so quickly at the Halifax refuelling, a lot of foam had been generated in the tanks and whilst we thought they were full of solid diesel fuel, some of the space must have been occupied by foam, and we hadn't in fact taken on board the full amount. The more immediate problem to solve was how to get to the next refuelling stop, and

we were faced with the alternative of going into St Johns in Newfoundland and getting fuel there—an action which would add a lot of time to the crossing or getting the refuelling ship to steam towards us. It was the latter course we adopted, but we were very conscious of the fact that this then increased the distance between the second and third refuelling stops—and this was the long ocean leg where there was very little margin to spare as far as fuel was concerned.

We made our rendezvous with the supply vessel which was to refuel us, still in fog. This supply vessel was operating in support of the semi-submersible drilling rig *Sedco 709*, which was drilling for oil on the Grand Banks. After tying up astern the fuel hoses were passed across, but a problem with the fuel pumps

Out on the Grand Banks the supply ship supporting the drilling rig Sedco 709 *had steamed towards us to conserve our remaining fuel supply.*

delayed the fuel transfer and we took 1½ hours to load the required amount here, being very careful to ensure that the tanks were properly full and that we had the right amount on board. Now we had been going for 36 hours and everybody was getting desperately tired. With the motion of the boat, sleep was very difficult and there was also the psychological block of now having to head out into the wild Atlantic, knowing that the fuel situation was very tight and we had a long stretch of open water to cover before the rendezvous with the refuelling ship in mid-Atlantic. More serious still, the weather forecast suggested a deteriortion in conditions instead of the expected fresh winds from the south which would have been on the beam, and would not have caused too much trouble. In fact, the wind was going to be from the south-east, taking us on the bow and offering us a very rapid period of encounter with the waves at our high speed of travel. In addition, as the fog cleared, we encountered violent electrical storms which lit up the Atlantic night with an awe-inspiring display of lightning. We were in no mood to appreciate this display, however, for the storm upset our electronic equipment and also cut off communication with our control centre in London. It was a very long and very tiring night and after battling on course for several hours we were gradually being slowed by the sea conditions. We made the decision to alter course towards the north-east in order to give a better ride and to enable us to make better progress. I think we were all very thankful when dawn finally broke, the wind eased and we passed out of the electrical storms. We were able to re-establish contact with London, but the feeling of relief brought by daylight was short lived, for when we checked the fuel situation we found that in the very difficult sea conditions, the boat had burned up more fuel than expected and once again we were faced with too little left in our tanks to make the next refuelling ship.

Even if the ship, the tug *Indomitable*, steamed towards us we would run out of fuel before the rendezvous could be made, and at this stage it looked as though we had blown any chance of establishing a new record on the Atlantic. Now, desperately tired and battered by the constant motion, this prospect was a depressing one. A ray of hope came when a Nimrod aircraft of the Royal Air Force appeared overhead. After making radio contact we explained our predicament and the pilot volunteered to go off and search the surrounding ocean to see if he could find a ship willing to let us have some fuel. It seemed a long shot, but within twenty minutes the aircraft was back with the good news that there was a ship just over the horizon prepared to stop and give us fuel.

Manoeuvering *Virgin Atlantic Challenger* alongside this huge container ship was a tricky operation and one of the radio antenna was damaged, but we got the three vital 45-gallon drums of fuel on board. Then, however, the fuel had to be transferred to the tanks by means of a hand pump, and we wasted about three hours on this operation, but at least

Above *Three 45-gallon oil drums of fuel are lowered from the container ship* Atlantic Cartier *in mid-Atlantic.*

Right *Tied up astern of the tug* Indomitable, *still 1,000 miles from the Bishop Rock.*

we had the vital fuel and could head on in the calmer seas towards *Indomitable*. A rendezvous here in late afternoon and a slick refuelling operation saw us on our way again, but the fuel situation was still not comfortable because *Indomitable* had steamed many miles to the west to rendezvous with us and thus it seemed likely that there would not be sufficient fuel to make the final leg to the Bishop Rock Lighthouse. This depressing thought and the desperate tiredness was moderated only by the fact that our timing suggested there was still a slim chance of getting the record. Now it was the job of the London control centre to try to arrange for a further refuelling stop as we continued our remorseless way eastwards. The engines kept up their steady beat, but once more the weather was turning foul. Out there in the lonely Atlantic we all wondered whether we could cope with another night of battering as the wind freshened again, but at least now the wind and seas were behind us. This was the weather we had expected and anticipated—being able to maintain speed in following sea conditions. However, we hadn't bargained for the wind to be quite so strong and after another very long night of battering and crashing through the waves, dawn showed that a considerable sea was running as we approached the southern Irish coast. By this time we were more desperately tired than ever. The motion of the boat made sleep nearly impossible, but still we fought our way to the east and we were still in with a chance of making the record, despite the delays caused by the fuel problems.

The London control centre had worked wonders in finding a ship prepared to give us further fuel. The Royal Navy auxiliary ship *Green Rover* was just 250 miles out from the Bishop Rock when we made a rendezvous with her. We were more than grateful not only for the fuel they passed across, but for the hot food and drinks which made a welcome addition to our very basic provisions carried on board. Now we could set our sights for the Bishop Rock Lighthouse with a good chance that the record was in our grasp, and our flagging spirits started to rise dramatically. By this time, however, the wind was blowing at Force 6 from the west and the sea was building up all the time. We were going to have a rough ride into the finish and we tried to find the most comfortable speed at which the boat would operate under these conditions. I calculated that a speed of 38½ knots ought to be adequate to reach the Bishop Rock within the record time and possibly even give us a couple of hours to spare, so we set off with renewed hope in our hearts.

As the sea built up the boat would climb over the back of a wave before crashing down the front again into the trough and then up the other side once more in what seemed to be a never-ending succession of waves. We were making good progress despite the conditions and we could see the record within our grasp. Now we were listening to every beat of the mighty diesels which had performed impeccably on the whole crossing and we were getting continual calls over the radio from the press and television to give interviews. We were just starting to bask in the glory of what we were about to achieve when disaster struck.

Coming over the back of a wave, we dropped yet once more into the trough but this time there was a noticeable bang, slightly louder than all the other bangs which were taking place. We didn't take too much notice straight away until we suddenly saw water pouring out from the continuously running bilge pump outlet, a sight which clearly spelt trouble. This meant that water was coming into the hull and we could already sense the boat getting sluggish. When we opened up the hatches to see what the problem was, there was already 3 ft of water in the starboard sponson and we knew that our race was run. The boat was taking on water rapidly, faster than the pumps could cope with. There seemed little we could do except prepare to abandon ship. Whether we had hit something or whether the hull had just given up, we didn't know, but now the boat was stopped we could see just how big the waves were and with darkness coming on we turned our minds to survival. Our radio link with the outside world was fading fast as the batteries went under water but I was able to send

out a distress message while the rest of
the crew were getting the life-rafts ready.
When it became obvious that the boat
wouldn't stay afloat much longer we
climbed into the life-rafts and drifted off
a little way, watching *Virgin Atlantic
Challenger* slowly sink. It was like watching an old friend die, this boat that we
had lived with and worked with for the
last six months. Now just 138 miles from
the Bishop Rock Lighthouse, the boat
was sinking and we were alone on the
ocean with the imminent prospect of
becoming another Atlantic casualty
statistic, as darkness was falling.

Right *Another victim of the Atlantic. Watching*
Virgin Atlantic Challenger *sink was like watching
an old friend die.*

Below *Richard Branson and Chay Blyth in the liferaft
with the first aeroplane overhead.*

Strangely I remember a great sense of relief that the banging and crashing had stopped, but I also remember thinking that if we were not found before it got dark, we might at the very best have a long lonely night in the life-rafts. However, word about our predicament had got through and within thirty minutes the first aircraft was overhead, the press aeroplane, busy taking photographs, and then came the friendly Nimrod. After that it was a fairly simple matter for a passing ship to be directed towards us. The *Geest Bay* carried out a superb bit of seamanship in getting alongside the two tiny life-rafts floating in the ocean. It can have been no easy task to manoeuvre a 10,000-ton ship in such strong winds and as we climbed the gangway dressed in survival suits and lifejackets we were met at the top by a steward carrying a tray of brandy glasses!

It was a wonderful return to civilization and normality as the Captain and crew of the *Geest Bay* offered us hospitality in the true traditions of the sea. Unaware of the drama we had created by sinking so close to the Bishop Rock Lighthouse with the record almost in our grasp, we were well looked after on board until a Royal Air Force Sea King helicopter came to lift us off the decks and take us ashore. It was a strange sensation flying above the ocean upon which so very recently we had been crashing along in *Virgin Atlantic Challenger*. We had actually crossed the Atlantic within the record time achieved by the SS *United States*, but our vessel had not and so we had failed. The press

and television of the world had been waiting for our arrival and now they wanted the story of our disaster. Surrounded by a huge battery of cameras we had to relate our experiences of the trip, and then it was once more back into the helicopter and on to food and warm beds and more interviews with press and television.

We had come so close to genuinely breaking the record for the fastest crossing held by the SS *United States*: indeed we had broken one record held by that great liner. In the first 24 hours of our record attempt we had covered a greater distance at sea than any other vessel afloat, nearly 1,000 miles. We had also achieved, or so it seemed, the most publicized sinking of any vessel in the Atlantic since the *Titanic*—although fortunately we were better prepared than the *Titanic*'s passengers and crew. But that Atlantic record had eluded us, and within days of getting ashore and recovering from the ordeal of the crossing, the first basic commitment to making another attempt was being made.

By coming so close we had at least demonstrated that it was possible to break this Atlantic record with a small boat, and the experience was not to be wasted. It showed, if further proof was needed, that you can't take anything for granted on the Atlantic. Richard Branson is not noted for giving up easily, and I think that once we had dried out and collected our thoughts we were all keen to get to grips with the Atlantic ocean once more. That chance came the following year.

A new Atlantic record

I was both excited and apprehensive at the prospect of making a second attempt on the Atlantic record. There was a tremendous excitement about the idea of building on our experience from the first disastrous crossing. The idea of having a second crack at the elusive speed record, which had stood for 35 years, was something that got all of us involved in the project very excited. The knowledge of the severe physical and mental pounding which we had experienced during our earlier attempt was never far from the back of my mind, and all of us must have considered whether we could, or even wanted to, stand up to that sort of punishment all over again. It was rather like the thought of going to the dentist, but knowing that the dental treatment was going to last for three days—and that wasn't an attractive prospect.

However, the possibility of starting from scratch with a blank sheet of paper to design a new boat was something which nobody turns down willingly, and the actual crossing was still a long way off. In the previous attempt the administration had been rather rambling and top heavy, partly due to the fact that two

major companies were involved. For this new attempt, Virgin Atlantic intended to go it alone as far as the sponsorship was concerned, and this made the administration and the decisions much easier. Time was certainly not on our side, however, for although the basic decision to go ahead had been made fairly soon after we stopped ashore from the previous trip, just getting the money and the organization together took time and then the boat had to be designed and built within the space of about six months— a very tall order indeed.

It was a situation which called for very tight administration and this was the first thing that had to be set up. Chris Witty, who worked for Cougar at the time, had come in rather late in the day as coordinator for the first record attempt, but now he switched over to Virgin and was appointed Project Director. Chris's background is mainly in motor racing, having handled public relations for the Toleman Formula One team, but whilst perhaps lacking in the nautical skills, there was no doubt about his administrative capabilities. The design of the new boat was put in the hands of Sonny Levi, probably one of

Above Virgin Atlantic Challenger II *takes shape at Brooke Yachts in Lowestoft.*

Below *The route across the Atlantic.*

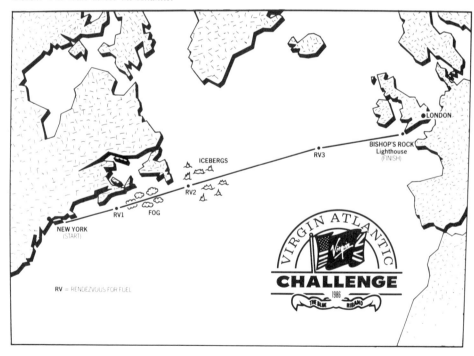

the most renowned and experienced fast boat designers in the world. Whilst Sonny drew the lines of the boat and had overall responsibility for the design, much of the structural design of the new hull and the day to day supervision of the construction was put in the hands of Peter Birkett. Peter had been responsible for most of the design of the first boat, but at the end of that project he had left Cougar Marine to set up as a freelance designer and this was his first project. On the engine side, Pete Downie who had put the machinery together for the first boat also came into this new project. This was the basic three-man team who lived with the boat from start to finish. I came in with responsibility for the electronics package on board which would cover navigation and communication. The four of us involved in this project were all professionals, highly motivated and experienced. During the building of this boat we managed to transfer a tremendous enthusiasm for this project to all the builders and suppliers who became involved, and it was this enthusiasm which had a lot to do with the successful and rapid construction of the boat.

The contract for building the boat went to Brooke Yachts in Lowestoft. Brooke Yachts is a subsidiary of Brooke Marine who had considerable experience in building fast patrol boats, but up to the time when they started work on *Virgin Atlantic Challenger II* they had little experience in aluminium construction. However, they were willing to learn, and during the last few months of 1985 the hull of *Virgin Atlantic Challenger II* took shape rapidly in a covered building shed at Lowestoft. With the building work underway it was time to look at the crew for this new attempt, and there was little doubt in everybody's mind that the numbers had to be reduced. On the first attempt a nine-man crew had proved far too many, particularly with the restricted space available on board, and this time we decided to limit numbers to six. Heading up the crew was Richard Branson in the role of skipper. He was backed up by an experienced team mainly drawn from the previous crew. Chay Blyth was back once more and I was again in the team as navigator and communicator. Steve Ridgway had demonstrated his skills as a fast boat driver and he came back into the project in this role. This second time around, Pete Downie would be in the crew as engineer, his experience in carrying out all the installation work on the engines being extremely valuable when the boat was at sea. Finally, Peter McCann would be back with his TV camera and also as an active crew member. This then was the chosen crew, and as we had all worked together before there was little need for the intensive training and familiarization which we had to go through the previous year.

The boat designed for this new attempt was a monohull rather than a catamaran. The limited design and building time available was the main reason for this choice. A vast bank of experience in monohull design exists and Sonny Levi was confident that he could produce a boat which would do the job without the need for the extensive trials and development work which had been required on the catamaran. The simpler construction of a monohull also reduced the building time, and I think that most of us also felt more comfortable with a more conventional monohull design. The same type of engines were to be used for this boat—the twelve-cylinder MTU diesels—but this time the manufacturers found 10 per cent more horsepower so that the load carrying ability would be slightly less critical than previously. We also hoped to get another two or three knots out of the boat with this extra power available. Surface propellers were again selected as the propulsion system, but these were to be incorporated into the newly developed Levi Drive—a bolt-on surface propeller drive system designed by Sonny Levi and built in Italy. This drive incorporates the propeller, the rudder and the engine exhaust system in one unit, the unique feature of which is the semicircular rudder which fits over and around the propeller, to give improved efficiency. The engine exhausts exit immediately in front of the top half of the propeller helping the water to break away from the transom area and, we hoped, avoiding the early problems we experienced on the first boat.

We spent a lot of time looking at the wheelhouse design and layout, because there is no doubt that the cramped conditions of the first boat were one of the major causes of the discomfort that we experienced. This time we had a lot more space to play with and we were able to build a mock-up in which we could install all the equipment, just to make sure that it could be operated efficiently even

under difficult conditions and that crew members who were resting would not be disturbed by the activities of the duty watch.

On the electronic side we went back to the same equipment which had proved reliable on the previous crossing, with the twin Rascal colour radars and two Skanti HF radios. Two radios were installed because of the need to maintain reliable communications, one being dedicated to telephone links and the other to telex operations. In the telex operation we could receive messages automatically on a printer, which avoided the need to write down complicated messages—a task which I had found very difficult on the violently moving boat. For position fixing, three primary units were installed, two Racal MNS 2000 receivers and a Trimble combined Loran and GPS satellite system. The Racal units incorporate satnav, Loran C, Decca Navigator and Omega, and so we were well provided with information. Having three independent units ensured that if one started to give false readings, it could be quickly recognized by comparing it with the other two. In the event, the position finding equipment proved the least reliable of all the systems on board, and out of the three installed only one was working at the end of the voyage.

Every little detail on board the boat had to be worked out very carefully, not only to ensure high standards of reliability, but also to give us a practical boat which could take on the Atlantic and this time survive to the finish line. We took a fresh look at all the safety systems and

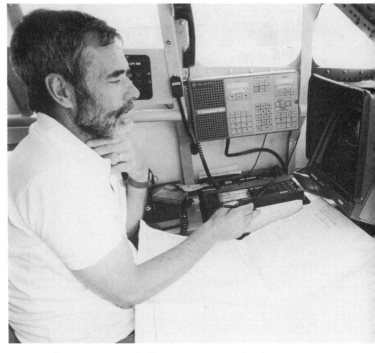

installed flotation bags to ensure that whatever happened, this time the boat wouldn't sink. Personal survival was also looked at in the light of our previous experiences, and I think we were all very proud of the boat which finally took to the water in April 1986. I remember vividly the day when the engines on *Virgin Atlantic Challenger II* were first fired up and all the dockyard workers at Brooke Marine turned out to see the boat go off to sea for the first time. I had the privilege of driving the boat on this first occasion and I don't think I have ever known a boat feel so right on its first outing. As soon as we left harbour we took the boat over the measured mile off Lowestoft and recorded a speed of 47 knots, which was very close to what we

expected. On our return to harbour, we were delighted with the performance of the boat and confident now that we could meet the tight deadlines necessary for an attempt to be made that coming summer.

The naming ceremony, during which Princess Michael of Kent once more broke the traditional champagne bottle across the vessel's bows, brought a huge gathering of personalities, sponsors and well wishers to Lowestoft, bringing the boat and its operations firmly into the public gaze. After the highly publicized sinking the year before, most of the movements of the boat were now followed by the lenses of TV and press cameras, in addition to the *Tomorrow's World* film crew who almost

Virgin Atlantic Challenger II *on trials.*

lived with us in order to get the material for the documentary they were once again producing on the project. Extensive trials over the measured mile and out in the North Sea were necessary in order to fine tune the propellers and to make sure that the boat would operate with a full load of fuel on board. Six huge fuel tanks made by Marston Palmer would hold a total of 12½ tonnes of diesel and we were delighted when, with this full fuel load on board, the boat still proved capable of achieving 47 knots. Running light the speed went up to 52 knots. Running in the rough seas of the North Sea the boat proved remarkably well-mannered in difficult conditions and we felt confident of the boat's ability to take the record.

After a farewell party, *Virgin Atlan-*

tic Challenger II finally left Lowestoft on the proving voyage round to Liverpool from where, like her ill-fated predecessor, she was to be shipped out to the USA. The first stop on this trip was at London and the two-hour passage there was made in winds of near gale force. This stop was to contribute to the Sport Aid festivities on the River Thames, then after this light relief we got down to the serious business of driving the boat. After a stop at Brighton we ran down the Channel to Plymouth. Coming round Start Point on our way into Plymouth, we had all become a bit relaxed because the boat was running so well and behaving almost faultlessly when suddenly we hit a couple of big waves in succession in the tide race off the headland. The boat flew into the air just as Pete Downie was coming out of the engine hatch. He also flew into the air and when he landed on the boat again, he broke his ankle. We quickly diverted into Salcombe to get medical help, but I think that Pete was more frustrated than hurt by this accident, since it would stop him coming with us on the Atlantic crossing. It was a major setback in our plans, because Pete knew the workings of the machinery intimately and he was going to be a difficult man to replace. Eventually the engine manufacturers agreed to let Eckhart Rastig who had supervised the installation on behalf of MTU, come with us as onboard engineer for the crossing. During the building we had all got to know Eckie very well and whilst we were very sad to lose Pete, Eckie, despite his funny accent made a good team member.

After being weather bound in Plymouth for two days while gales roared in from the Atlantic, we finally nosed out round Land's End to a refuelling exercise rendezvous with the Irish Navy ship *Aiofe*. This ship would be waiting for us out in mid-Atlantic when we made our dash across the ocean and the exercise confirmed that all systems were working well. By mid-day we had completed the exercise to our satisfaction and also talked to a friendly Nimrod aircraft which was once more flying overhead. After that it was full speed up the Irish Sea to Liverpool where *Virgin Atlantic Challenger II* was packed up and put on board the Atlantic Container Line's ship bound for Halifax in Nova Scotia.

Now the pace was truly starting to hot up. We had done all we could, building and testing the boat to the highest standards possible: now it was up to the crew to get their act together and for the study of the Atlantic weather to begin. *Virgin Atlantic Challenger II* was off-loaded in Halifax because we wanted to get more experience with the boat in the waters in which she would have to operate, and the intention was to drive her the 600 miles to New York as a further trial. Leaving Halifax late at night, we had a rough passage down the coast of Nova Scotia before heading into Boston to pick up Richard Branson and to meet the American press for the first time. Then it was down through the Cape Cod canal and Long Island Sound to New York. Here we had thick fog for most of the route and some very unpleasant sea conditions in the narrow waters of Long Island Sound. This eighteen-hour run gave us some good experience but also a warning of the difficult times to come.

Once again New York took us in with open arms, with the traditional fireboat welcome and parties, but we had to knuckle down to the hard work of the final preparations and watching the movements of the weather. Our base once more was in Mamaroneck, and this time to help us with the weather forecasting we had Peter Deekes, an experienced meteorologist. The weather maps came in over the fax machine from the Meteorological Office in Bracknell. We had the benefit of the latest computer technology in these weather maps and they even gave three-day forecasts of waves and swell. Every morning and evening we would study the charts closely, looking for the break which would signal our departure, and almost immediately we were aware that the weather patterns in 1986 were much better than those we had seen the previous year.

After only ten days there were hopeful signs that we might get away fairly soon, the one problem being a depression which was more or less static just to the west of Ireland. On the American side of the ocean we were enjoying fine weather but there were regular disturbances moving out into the Atlantic in the Newfoundland area. On 25 June, the depression over Ireland began to disintegrate and we got the break we were looking for. Final preparations were made with the boat, and the two remaining crew, Richard Branson and Chay Blyth, were summoned from

England. When he received the message, Richard Branson was having lunch with Prince Charles and he had to make his excuses in order to catch the aeroplane to be in New York ready for the departure early the following morning. Having made the decision to go, I can remember feeling very worried about whether I had got the right weather window. Would the depression over Ireland really break up as forecast? Should we have waited a little longer? Then I was equally concerned about a depression which was coming across North America and which would close down the weather window for several days if we didn't take the opportunity offered. It was a narrow gap in the weather, but you can't afford the luxury of waiting for calms all the way. The chance that was offered was still a gamble, but we had to take it.

Four o'clock on the morning of 26 June saw final preparations being made under the glare of television lights at the boatyard in Mamaroneck. There was a great felling of *déjà-vu* as we set off once more down the East River to a final farewell before the press and television at New York's Water Club. Dawn was breaking as we headed out past the Statue of Liberty to the Ambrose Light Tower. On this second attempt there was none of the excitement and anticipation which I had felt on the first departure, rather a feeling of resignation and hope that I had made the right decisions. These weighed heavily on my shoulders, but the early morning sun held out the promise of a fine day and as we roared over the start line at 6.00 am conditions

Virgin Atlantic Challenger II *leaves New York at the start of the record run.*

were absolutely perfect, our only cause for complaint being the sun in our eyes as we headed east.

Immediately after departure we established radio contact with the control centre in the Virgin Megastore in London, set up as previously, but this time with the addition of a back-up navigator in the form of Dr Rob Howarth, who would look at all the options open to us in the light of changes in the weather and sea conditions as we went across. This time we had introduced the possibility of deviating from our chosen route to a certain extent, if this would help us get better sea conditions. In the event this proved a very valuable addition to our plans. Once this contact was made we could settle down

to the routine of running the boat, splitting the watches of two on and two off, whilst myself and Eckie were available as required for our specialist duties. It is amazing in this situation how quickly you adapt to the circumstances in which you find yourself, and very soon we had established our own little microcosm of civilization out there in the Atlantic, seemingly far removed from everything else that was happening in the world. No doubt many other Atlantic voyagers in small craft had done the same thing, but we found it still happened despite the fact that we were continually in touch with London. The radio link does not intrude into your own world out there on the ocean.

The engines maintained a steady

beat as we roared our way eastward towards the Nantucket Shoals at speeds approaching 50 knots. It was certainly wonderful to have these conditions at the start and it gave us a great opportunity to settle down, but no sooner had we settled into a routine then the first drama occurred.

This took the form of a whale which suddenly surfaced right in front of the boat, no more than 100 yards away. The problem of having a whale surface in front of you is that you have no indication which way it is travelling, but we must have made the right guess because rapid avoiding action allowed the whale to pass close down the side of the boat, close enough in fact for us to smell it. The event shook us out of our complacency and we sighted two more whales, although a bit further off than the first one, before we arrived at Nantucket Island for the delicate navigation operation through the shoals. There was an anxious moment going through here when he saw broken water right across our course line, which could have been

shoal water or could have been a tide rip. Fortunately it proved to be the latter and we ploughed on still keeping up speed close to 50 knots and then headed out on the far side, setting a course for the first refuelling stop off Halifax.

By midday the sun had disappeared and the wind was freshening and we had to ease speed back to 44 knots, but we were comfortably ahead of our schedule and this time there was no sign of the dreaded fog. In fact the trip was almost boring because of the lack of incident, and it was only the regular contacts with London over the radio which provided a break in the monotony. It is amazing how quickly you can get used to travelling at high speeds so that they appear quite normal. Everything on board was functioning well, although before arrival at the first refuelling stop that afternoon the first of the position finding systems went totally dead. Whilst the other two were working well this was not of too much concern, and we found the refuelling ship without a problem.

An awkward swell was building up

Above left *Passing the Ambrose Light Tower at the start.*

Above *Coming alongside at the first refuelling stop off Halifax.*

Right *Richard Branson and Steve Ridgeway at the steering position.*

from the south-east as we approached the first refuelling ship off Halifax and this indicated that our honeymoon with the weather was over. We could now look forward to more uncomfortable conditions for the remainder of the crossing as we had expected from the forecast, which was turning out to be very accurate so far. This first refuelling took longer than anticipated, but we were on our way again before nightfall, this time aiming to pass some fifteen miles south of Cape Race on the Great Circle route. This would take us to the second refuelling stop at the same drilling rig as before, although now drilling a new area some fifty miles to the south. Reports had suggested that there were six icebergs in the area south of Cape Race and we set a course to pass clear of their reported position, but you hever can tell with the movement of icebergs and we were relieved that there was still no fog about, although visibility was down to less than five miles. Nothing showed up on the radar and we continued on out into the Atlantic past Cape Race, passing close to the shallow Virgin Rocks and on towards the rendezvous with the *Nordetor*, the supply vessel dancing attendance on the drilling rig.

Over the Grand Banks the swell was coming at us from two directions, giving '*Challenger*' a very unpredictable and bumpy ride which was particularly tiring and taxing. The adrenalin which had kept us going for the first 24 hours was wearing off rapidly and it became a matter of sheer hard work and concentration to perform the necessary tasks to keep the boat on course and on schedule.

By midday the sea had flattened out a little, much to everyone's relief, but it was replaced by fog patches, so once more we were glued to the radar screen, and it was with considerable relief that we saw the *Nordetor* appear out of the dense fog just 300 yards away, with all lights blazing. At this stage we were still ahead of schedule and apart from the uncomfortable ride, the crossing was going well. Tied up astern of the *Nordetor*, the refuelling was carried out quickly and efficiently—or so we thought—and with nearly half of the distance behind us, we looked forward to an uncomfortable but predictable run across the remainder of the ocean to snatch the record from the SS *United States*. Although tired, we were all feeling quite pleased with ourselves: the boat was behaving almost faultlessly and the experience which had gone into the planning was paying off. Then the gremlins struck.

When we came to fire up the engines after casting off from the *Nordetor*, nasty noises and clouds of smoke indicted trouble: water had contaminated the fuel. The problem was quickly identified by the engineers but took agonizing hours to solve. In taking on fresh fuel from the *Nordetor*, we had also unintentionally received nearly four tonnes of water. The water settled into the bottom of the tanks and the engines refused to run on the mixture. The only answer was to drain the whole system and then take on fresh fuel. The system had never been designed for draining in this way, and it meant disconnecting pipes at the bottom of the fuel tanks and letting the

Refuelling from the Nordetor *on the Grand Banks.*

fuel and water mixture run into the bilges from where it could be pumped out. For the engineers it was a nightmare operation in the constantly moving boat. They were soon covered from head to toe in diesel fuel and the whole boat became a sliding, slippery skating rink. Work went on for hour after painful hour with the record prospects disappearing equally quickly. Finally the worst of the water had been removed, and we could fire up the engines again and tie up on the stern of the *Nordetor* to take on fresh fuel.

By midnight we were topped up and ready to go again, but we had to take a careful look at our situation. The delay had upset the weather sequence we might expect and a severe storm was coming up behind us. It was this storm which persuaded us that we would be better to head to the east out across the Atlantic rather than head back into the safety of St Johns and abandon the record attempt. At this stage we were not at all happy about the reliability of the engines because a considerable amount of water still remained in the fuel system. The fuel tanks comprised large blocks of foam surrounded by a rubber skin, and whilst this foam would let the diesel fuel through quickly, it tended to hold the water, and we knew that we were likely to have continual problems with water passing through the fuel systems. In the end we decided to keep going, and to help us with the machinery problems we took on board an extra crew member in the form of Steve Lawes who had been our refuelling manager on board the *Nordetor*.

This was a very wise move because within half an hour of leaving we were stopped once more to allow the fuel filters to be drained of water. This became a recurring problem hour after hour as we battered our way eastwards. The two engineers became very adept at clearing the water, but none the less it was a delaying process not helped by the fact that the water in the fuel was steadily ruining the paper fuel filters themselves and we were rapidly running out of spares. Adding to our problems were the deteriorating sea conditions. As we went further east, an unpredicted north-easterly swell arose to slow our progress. Things were looking fairly black and it was clear tht if we were going to have any chance of taking the Atlantic record we would have to fight for it every inch of the way. Furthermore large patches of fog kept us glued to the radar screens, and our complacency on the early stages of the crossing was now replaced by a desperate battle to keep up speed as the schedule fell behind.

Our most immediate worry was running out of fuel filters and this concern was transmitted to Tim Powell, running the control centre. He managed to organize a canister with spares to be loaded on board a Nimrod aircraft which was out on exercise and which located us in mid-ocean. The Nimrod was always a welcome sight overhead, a reassurance that there is a world going on outside, and they did a wonderful job in dropping the canister just fifty yards ahead of the boat. We quickly recovered it, very grateful now to have spare filters available. But the north-easterly swell was still building up and we were gradually having to ease back the speed—first to 36 knots and then right down to 33 knots and as darkness fell on this third night we were beginning to feel depressed about the situation for we were literally running out of time to set a new record. We were also suffering quite considerably with the violent movement of the boat which had developed a tendency to fly off the top of the developing swell. The second of the position finding systems now chose to pack up and the third one did not appear to be providing particularly reliable information, which meant that we were now heading across the Atlantic on dead reckoning yet still with the vital rendezvous with the third refuelling ship in mid-Atlantic to be made with pinpoint accuracy. This was causing me a lot of concern, but fortunately we made radio contact with this ship when over 100 miles away and they were able to provide us with radio bearings so that we could home in on her.

It was midnight before we came up to the *Aiofe* with her lights blazing in the

Above *The Nimrod aircraft dropping the canister with new fuel filters.*

Right *Recovering the canister from the water.*

middle of the Atlantic. It was a welcome sight and despite the heavy swell and the difficult conditions, they did a remarkably efficient job of passing the fuel across. They also provided us with some excellent hot Irish stew which revived our flagging spirits and within half an hour, we were off on the final 750 miles to the Bishop Rock.

There was still a chance that we could get the record, if only we could keep going at a fair speed. Whilst we were battling our way to the *Aiofe* the control centre in London had been having a close look at the situation. They advised that we take on a full load of fuel in order to keep the boat sitting well in the water and reduce the amount it might fly in the heavy swell. More importantly, they advised that we follow an alternative route to the Bishop Rock, which ought to keep us clear of the worst of the difficult sea conditions. By heading further south we could skirt round the depression over Ireland which hadn't broken up to the extent that had been expected. The south-easterly course would put the north-easterly swell on the beam and enable us to keep a higher speed. Thus when we left the *Aiofe* we headed south-east for 400 miles powering our way through the pitch black night, still on dead-reckoning, in a desperate bid to make up time.

I will remember that night for a long time to come as we drove the boat for all it was worth. Steve Ridgway was on the helm most of the night trying to strike the delicate balance between driving the boat as hard as possible yet preventing it from flying off the top of waves. It was

a difficult task in the dark and the boat crashed and thundered its way towards the Bishop Rock with a crew fighting to stay in control. All nights have to come to an end and there was welcome relief all round when dawn appeared to the east, enabling us to see the adversary we had struggled against all night. Daylight enabled us to drive the boat using the throttles and to raise the speed by a couple of knots. By now we had been on the boat for three days and three nights and we were all desperately tired. The strain was beginning to tell in many little ways, but we were all buoyed up by the prospect that even after all the difficulties we had experienced, we might still just crack the record. At daylight we once again saw the friendly Nimrod which was able to give us a useful check on our position. This enabled me to pick up the signals from the European Decca Navigator system, and once more I was able to plot the progress of the boat with accuracy.

Throughout that morning we managed to keep the speed in excess of 40 knots and calculations showed that we could probably just break the record if only we could keep going. Now we were listening to every beat of the engines as we altered course directly towards the Bishop Rock, hoping that everything would hold together. By midday it became obvious that someone was praying on our behalf as there was an almost miraculous change in the weather. Within half an hour the swell which had caused us so much trouble had died down and the grey skies turned to blue. This gave a wonderful boost to our flagging spirits and from somewhere we dragged up hidden reserves of energy to brace ourselves for the final couple of hundred miles.

Now the speed could be increased to 50 knots and all that afternoon we powered our way to the east, in constant communication with London and with frequent requests for radio and television interviews. We were conscious of a growing excitement in the outside world as the record looked increasingly possible, but even at this late stage the Atlantic did not relent and once more the sea conditions began to deteriorate to the point where we were having to ease back on the throttles again. There was precious little time to spare and we were fighting a difficult battle to remain alert and to keep the boat running at its best speed. We were all too well aware of having been through this same situation before, only to experience the boat sinking underneath us so close to home. Nobody spoke very much at all as we approached the point where the original *Virgin Atlantic Challenger* had sunk, and I think we half expected its ghost to rise out of the water right in our tracks.

There was a great feeling of relief when we passed that milestone and faced the final three-hour run to the lighthouse and the finish. All we had to do now was keep going and we would have the record broken by a good two hours.

Finally the radar screen showed up a target just thirteen miles away—the Bishop Rock Lighthouse. Now we could almost row the boat to the finish line, but still things were not easy. An ominously large target appeared on the radar screen and transformed itself into a huge and violent rain squall which swept in across our track. The rain itself didn't worry us, but it cut down the visibility to less than one mile, and, more worrying still, it blotted out the lighthouse on the radar screen. We were heading blind at close to 50 knots towards the rocks off the Scilly Isles and all eyes strained ahead desperately to pick out the lighthouse in the gloom. We knew we were close when welcoming helicopters started to fly overhead and then suddenly, there it was. The grey sombre finger of the lighthouse identified by its powerful light loomed up just a mile and a half away out of the rain and we knew we had made it. We saw the flotilla of welcoming boats, but with the throttles hard on the stops we concentrated on the run to the finish line.

Suddenly it was all over and we had broken the record by just over two hours.

It was a wonderful moment, a moment to savour, but we were rapidly surrounded by the welcoming boats and there was no time for any private thoughts. After catching our breath and posing for photographs in the still pouring rain we once more opened the throttles and headed round for St Mary's where a vast flotilla waited to welcome us into harbour. It was a wonderful welcome from this seafaring community which has seen so much drama at the end of Atlantic crossings. We were the first speed record holders to call in at St Mary's, as the liners had always passed disdainfully on up channel to land their passengers. It seemed as though every one on the island had

Above *Celebrations alongside at St Mary's in the Scilly Islands.*

Left *Approaching the Bishop Rock Lighthouse at the end of the record run.*

turned out to greet us. The champagne flowed and the welcome was all too much for our bruised and battered minds and bodies. Two years of planning and plotting had gone into this instant and our victory changed the pattern of Atlantic records. For the first time ever the Atlantic speed record was held by a boat rather than a ship, and this was also the first time that diesel power had been used to set an Atlantic record. The diminutive 4,000 hp *Virgin Atlantic Challenger II* may look tiny in comparison with the massive 1,000 ft long SS *United States* with its 250,000 hp, but my goodness, we'd taken her record!

After the crossing was over, many pundits argued that ours was not a true Atlantic record because we had to refuel on the way. I would argue that it is the time of the crossing which counts, not so much the method, and anyway, many of the early steamships which claimed Atlantic records had used their sails to help them across. The boat in which we had set a new Atlantic record was about the same length as that used by Columbus on his pioneering Atlantic crossing. I like to think that in its own way, our crossing was also a pioneering one. It showed that with the death of the high speed Atlantic liner through changing circumstances, there are alternative ways of setting new records. Others will no doubt follow in our footsteps and as Richard Branson said after the crossing, 'We throw down the gauntlet to others and we wish them well.'

The challenge remains

Time hasn't mellowed the Atlantic. Even today with advanced marine technology and all the resources of tank testing, research and development and modern weather forecasting there is nothing certain about the ever changing waters of the Atlantic. Modern ships built to the highest standards still find themselves in difficulty, and even the wonders of modern radar have not entirely removed the risk of collision between ships or with icebergs.

The Atlantic is a safer place than it was 100 years ago, but only because safety standards and communications have improved. Ship and boat casualties are more of a rarity these days, but newspaper reports still tell of large well found ships coming to grief in stormy waters through cargo shifting or, perhaps, through structural failure. Small boats as well, despite improvements in their construction, are still having to reckon with the awesome power of Atlantic waves and weather, and the risks remain.

One problem is that advances in technology are not always used to provide additional margins of safety. Safety standards tend to remain static, whilst new technology is used initially to commercial advantage—to make ships more efficient for carrying passengers or cargo. The margins in shipping these days are very small and the competition is as intense as ever. While safety does not necessarily take second place, there is certainly no leeway left in most commercial operations for safety margins to be increased over and above that demanded by the regulations. Regulations themselves can often be far from perfect and so accidents continue to happen and tragedies occur. In small boats where the commercial pressures do not exist, speed tends to be the major factor and advanced technology is used to further this cause first and only secondly to make sailing safer.

The yardstick for record breaking is now the all-comers time set by *Virgin Atlantic Challenger II* which crossed the Atlantic in 3 days 8 hours and 31 minutes. For sailboats the time to beat is the 7 days 12 hours 50 minutes record set by *Fleury Michon*. Both of these records are beatable but as speeds continue to rise, breaking the record becomes increasingly difficult because the margins become smaller. *Virgin*

Atlantic Challenger II wasted eight hours in the Atlantic sorting out her fuel problem, and so this boat could certainly set out to break its own record. Without that delay in mid-Atlantic, *Virgin Atlantic Challenger II* would have crossed the Atlantic in three days flat to achieve an average speed of around 40 knots. This must certainly be the speed to aim for in any future attempt, but it is never going to be easy and it will always require meticulous planning and a certain amount of luck.

The power record for the Atlantic crossing, so painfully built up over the years by the Atlantic liners and now being taken to higher levels by modern fast powerboats, is the *America*'s Cup of the powerboat world. The two attempts in *Virgin Atlantic Challengers I* and *II* demonstrated what could be achieved and it is this type of high profile project which can attract sponsors to the project. It is not a record for the faint-hearted— the three days of punishment even under 'good' conditions take a physical and a mental toll. Breaking the record is not simply a question of producing a superbly prepared boat with the required speed, it is a question of finding a crew who can cope with adversity, with pain and with protracted tension to steer the boat past the Bishop Rock in record time.

On the sailing front conditions are just as demanding and last for twice as long. Here too the skills involved stretch further than designing a strong, fast boat which can take on the Atlantic. It is necessary to find the right weather conditions over a seven-day period which will allow consistent high speeds. History has shown that many attempts on the Atlantic sailing record have foundered when the wind has died away just as the record appeared within grasping distance. Unlike powerboats the sailing craft need strong, even gale force winds to give them maximum speed, and whilst these seem to abound in the Atlantic, the problem is to find them consistently over the 3,000-mile route, and from the right direction. For this reason the record set by *Fleury Michon* may stand for longer than that established by *Virgin Atlantic Challenger II*. *Fleury Michon*'s time was amazingly fast but it would be unlikely if no-one will at least attempt to crack it, and Phillipe Poupon has forecast a 7-day crossing in the next few years.

Strangely enough the record set by the schooner *Atlantic* in 1906 still stands as the fastest *monohull* sailing boat crossing of the Atlantic. For eighty years now, no monohulled sailing boat has crossed the Atlantic faster, but a race due to be held this year may see this record finally broken. This race, the BOC Blue Riband Challenge is from Ambrose Light Tower to the Lizard in Cornwall and is open to monohulls only. It is open to two classes of boats: vessels ranging from 40-50 ft in length, and boats between 50-60 ft. Apart from the length restriction there are no limitations on the boat or rigs used. It will take an average speed of something over 10 knots to beat the *Atlantic*'s record and June is not necessarily a favourable month in terms of weather because winds may be lighter than at other times of the year.

On the powerboat side a number of projects have been announced with the objective of breaking the record established by *Virgin Atlantic Challenger II*. Italy was one of the first countries to announce a record attempt and a consortium, which included many of the top powerboat racing names in that country, was brought together for this project. The Italian venture plans to follow the route taken by Bob Magoon in 1977, setting off from Spain and heading out into the Atlantic via the Azores and then to a refuelling ship, before finishing in New York. This is the traditional route taken by the Italian liners on their record attempts although it is slightly longer than the northerly route followed by *Virgin Atlantic Challenger II*.

The boat design favoured by the project is a 78 ft vessel powered by twin Isotta Fraschini diesel engines. In design it does not sound very different from the pattern established by *Virgin Atlantic Challenger II* and the Italians are going for the tried and tested solution rather than anything revolutionary. The Italian project is heavily supported by the Italian government and industry but it has been slow to get underway and no announcement has yet been made about when the attempt might be made, although 1988, is the first possible date.

A similar concept is favoured by an American attempt on the record announced in 1986. This team, headed by Ben Kramer, the 1984 offshore racing world champion, plans to use a 65 ft GRP hull powered by twin GM diesels. Kramer runs Apache Powerboats in Florida and the 65 ft prototype design is planned as a fast cruiser in the Apache range of powerboats. This project will follow even more closely the pattern established by *Virgin Atlantic Challenger II* in that there will be three fuel stops on the way. Kramer and his team plan to cut between two and ten hours off the 1986 record. Although originally scheduled to take place in 1988 this record attempt has now been put back and it is unlikely to happen before 1989 at the earliest.

The same goes for a much more ambitious project which originated in Britain called *Atlantic Sprinter*. Developed by world land speed record holder Richard Noble in conjunction with powerboat designer Don Shead, this involves a boat of about 100 ft in length, powered by a main centreline gas turbine engine, driving a KaWeMa water jet unit. This main engine, which would produce around 6,000 hp, would be supported by two wing diesel engines also driving water jets which would be used for harbour manoevring and to provide maximum power to get the boat up on to the plane with a full fuel load. This all-British challenge will save time by having only one refuelling stop, and the larger size of the boat should give a smoother ride in more difficult weather conditions. This ambitious project which was also scheduled to make the crossing in 1988 has so far failed to attract a sponsor which again proves that raising the necessary money is more of a problem than finding volunteers to take on the ocean.

Ted Toleman, the initiator of the first *Virgin Atlantic Challenge* attempt, is also keen to enter the fray again. He has drawn up plans for a larger catamaran vessel, again powered by MTU diesels. This attempt would follow very closely the lines of the first *Virgin Atlantic Challenger* attempt, with the larger-sized, higher-powered craft giving a better ride in Atlantic wave conditions. Although the money was reportedly raised to get this project off the ground, the heavy workload currently going through the building shops at Cougar Marine has meant that the project has to be put off for at least a year, and there seems some doubt now as to whether it too will ever get to sea. Perhaps if the Italians or Americans take the record from Britain, then the motivation for British sponsors and another British attempt will be much stronger. National pride remains an important factor in Atlantic record setting.

The most advanced of all the projects which aim to challenge the record set by *Virgin Atlantic Challenger II* is that of US powerboat ace Tom Gentry. Gentry is having a boat built at the Bristol ship-yard of Vosper Thornycroft and plans to make an attempt on the Atlantic record in the summer of 1988. This 110 ft craft, which is being built from aluminium, has been designed by Peter Birkett who was responsible for the successful design of *Virgin Atlantic Challenger II*. It will be powered by twin V-16 MTU diesel engines each producing 2,500 hp which will give the boat a speed in excess of 50 knots. With this design, Gentry is opting for the tried and tested solution and with this there is every likelihood that he will succeed.

Other projects are looking at a more radical approach. In Holland, a team is building the *Spirit of Amsterdam*—which looks like a beer bottle supported on hydrofoils. This 36 ft long revolutionary design is powered by a single 870 hp GM diesel to give a projected speed of 45 knots. The big question mark with such a design is the behaviour of a small hydrofoil craft in Atlantic waves and, quite naturally, there is a lot of scepticism about such a project. Not quite so revolutionary is a three pointer design developed in France. This 100 ft long craft has a central hull to which are attached two side hulls at the stern which house the 2,500 hp engines and the water jet propulsion units.

The international nature of the competition on the Atlantic record is reflected in these projects. In addition there has been interest from Swedish, West German and other Italian and French teams, so perhaps a race across is an exciting challenge to anticipate over the next few years.

All of these projected attempts at the Atlantic record call for refuelling on the crossing in one form or another. Although *Virgin Atlantic Challenger II* has broken the stranglehold of the liners on the speed record, the next big challenge is to break the record without refuelling on the way. Such an attempt will really take marine technology right to the limits because it requires a very fine balance between the size and weight of the vessel against power and fuel consumption. It is doubtful whether anything under 100 ft in length could carry adequate fuel for the non-stop

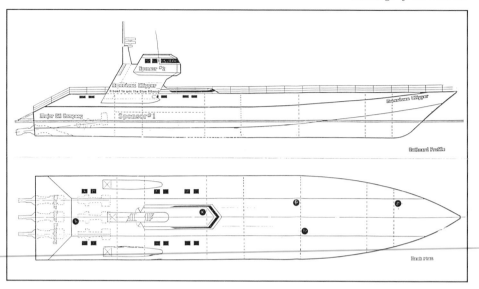

The American Clipper *is an ambitious design for a craft to take the Atlantic non-stop speed record for powerboats.*

crossing and with this size of vessel we are looking at enormous power requirements to get the maximum speed of 50 knots or more which will be required to set a new record. This means a very expensive vessel, but on the other hand the organization may be easier, in that dispensing with refuelling stops saves a lot of back-up and also reduces the risk element in the crossing, possibly raising the chances of success.

A team spearheaded by the famous Italian yacht builders Azimut/Benetti is developing such a project with the aim of making a record attempt in 1988. This boat will have a length of 95 ft and will be powered by four 1,800 hp CRM diesel engines. These diesels will be linked in pairs through a gearbox to two Riva Calzoni water jets to give a top speed in light condition of close to 60 knots. The boat will carry nearly twice its own weight in fuel to make the Atlantic crossing without a stop, but the tank tests have shown that the project is feasible.

A much more ambitious project for a non-stop record attempt is being developed in the USA. Some 198 ft in length and powered by three huge gas turbine engines, each producing 7,700 hp and linked to a water jet propulsion unit, this vessel is designed for construction in aluminium. It will have a dry weight of 400 tons and be able to carry 320 tons of fuel, sufficient to feed the hungry turbines for the 3,000 mile crossing. With a full fuel load, the top speed would be 45 knots, and when running light on fuel this would increase to 60 knots. This speed potential makes this vessel the fastest ship ever developed for the Atlantic crossing, and it would have the potential to make the passage at an average speed of 50 knots taking just 2½ days.

This is a very ambitious project, but also a very feasible one and it could have considerable commercial spin-off by demonstrating the basis of a potential warship design. Again the stumbling block is raising the necessary finance, but as virtually all of this is ploughed into the vessel rather than into the supporting requirements, there is every chance of recovering a high proportion of the investment following a successful crossing, by the sale of the boat. A project on this scale takes the Atlantic record out of the powerboat category once more and puts it back into the shipping world. The size of the vessel is similar to that of the first liners which mde the Atlantic crossing, although we are unlikely to see craft of this type carrying passengers on the Atlantic. Even though they offer a high speed potential, there is no way that such a craft could compete with the comfort and speed of aircraft which now dominate the Atlantic passenger-carrying trade.

There seems little prospect of significant numbers of passengers being carried across the Atlantic by ship in the future except for the current leisurely crossings made by cruise ships. In the future we may see large hovercraft and hydrofoils making very fast Atlantic crossings, but their potential will lie in military rather than commercial purposes.

The record for a non-stop powerboat crossing of the Atlantic remains at a miserly 7 or 8 knots. No planing boat has crossed the Atlantic except for Jim Wynne's attempt with the small outboard-powered *Coronet Express,* and that had to be carried part of the way and refuelled from the mother ship twice a day. Modern technology offers very lightweight construction and fuel efficient diesel engines which could offer a 45 ft vessel the potential of a non-stop crossing at 20 knots. This would at least bring the non-stop powerboat record up to the levels achieved by the sailing boats which hold the record for the fastest non-stop boat crossing of the Atlantic.

A 45 ft vessel capable of 20 knots is much more in the tradition of small boats on the Atlantic and in order to save every ounce of weight it would probably be sailed single-handed. This could be reasonably safe with modern electronics and radar and would be a fitting prelude to the non-stop record attempt being developed for the 198 ft vessel in the USA. This is a comparatively cheap record project and offers an interesting challenge to technology, endurance and reliability, features which have been the hallmark of attempts on Atlantic crossings throughout history. This is just one of many possible attempts to set new records and the Atlantic looks like remaining a busy place for record breakers and races in the years to come.

Index